# HOMO SAPIENS PART - X

## THE HEART OF HUMANITY: A BOOK OF EIGHTY POETIC MEDITATIONS

## MAWPHNIANG NAPOLEON

"To thee, dear readers, with mirth and glee,

This book doth dedicate its pages three.

Thou art the spark that sets its wit aglow,

The reason why its story doth flow.

In hopes that thou dost find delight,

In every word, each pun so bright.

So take this gift and revel in its glee,

And laugh thy fill, fair readers, for thee.

And if perchance, thou art of mirth bereft,

Fear not, for humor is what we've left.

So turn the page, and let the jest begin,

And we shall see, our book and thee shall win.

So here's a toast, to thee, our cherished friend,

With ink and paper, 'til the very end.

May this book bring joy and laughter to thine days,

And may its wit and humor light up thy ways.

And when thou hast perused each page with care,

Think not that our connection endeth there.

For in thy mind, our story shall endure,

And in thy heart, its humor shall assure.

So read on, dear reader, with a smile so bright,

And revel in the joy this book doth ignite.

For in its pages, thou wilt find delight,

And we shall be, eternally, bound in its light."

Warm regards,

A - Team

# Contents


*Foreword* — *xi*

*Preface* — *xiii*

*Acknowledgements* — *xv*

*Prologue* — *xvii*

1. Retribution's Resolve: A Sonnet Of Vindication — 1

2. The Paradox Of Perfection: A Sonnet — 6

3. Emancipation Through Torpor: A Sonnet Of Alacrity And Tranquility — 9

4. The Immeasurable Worth Sonnet — 13

5. Ode To Erudite Consequentialism — 16

6. Ethereal Introspection — 18

7. Fortitude's Flight: A Sonnet Of Solitude — 21

8. Eternal Embrace: A Sonnet Of Undying Love — 24

9. The Neoplasm Of The Cerebrum: A Cycle Of Desolation And Lamentations — 26

10. Nefelibata: A Sonnet Of Fantasia And Longing — 30

11. The Paradox Of Fortitude: A Maleficent Conundrum — 33

12. The Resilience Of Kongthei: A Tale Of Woe And Fortitude — 37

13. Nalagon Of Ataraxia: A Sonnet Of Longing And Serenity — 40

14. Melancholy's Haven: A Sonnet Of Domiciliary Disquietude — 42

15. Exaltation's Egress: A Sonnet Of Domestic Turmoil — 45

16. Sanguineous Sufferance: A Sonnet Of Phobia — 48

17. Nasal Nemesis: A Sonnet Of Suffering — 51

18. The Paradox Of Shylock: A Test Of Kismet — 53

19. Quantum Conundrum: A Mind's Befuddlement — 58

20. Perambulating Paddies: A Sonnet Of Syadheh — 63

# Contents


21. Christine De Pisan: The Trailblazer Of Women's Literature In 68
    Medieval Europe

22. Yuletide Descent: A Tragedy Of U Bah From Bhoi    71

23. The Elusive Quest: A Sonnet To The Omnipotent Creator    75

24. Reminiscence Of Imprisonment: A Sonnet    80

25. Ode To Sanguinity    83

26. Exasperation's Scourge: The Ineptitude Sonnet    86

27. Reminiscence Of Lost Youth    89

28. Triumph Through Perseverance: A Sonnet On Overcoming    91
    Adversity

29. The Onus Of Benevolence: A Sonnet    93

30. Botanical Fortitude: The Jeanne Baret Sonnet    96

31. Realms Unveiled: A Sonnet On Proprietorship And Autonomy 98

32. Eminence Through Effort: A Sonnet On The Process Of    100
    Attainment

33. The Proclivities Of Prosperity: A Sonnet Of Habits And    103
    Success

34. Purposeful Progression: A Sonnet On The Fear Of Death    106

35. Examining The Grandiloquence Of Wagner's Opus: A    108
    Philosophical Perspective On The Human Condition

36. Genuine Greatness: A Sonnet On The Elusiveness Of    112
    Authenticity

37. Dhanushkodi : A Sonnet    115

38. Nostalgia For The Lost Self: A Sonnet Of Self-reflection    116

39. The Ambition's Paradox: A Sonnet Of Grandiose Aspirations    119

40. The Conundrum Of Ethanol's Quantitude: A Sonnet Of    120

# Contents


Salubrity

41. The Paradox Of The Mind: A Sonnet Of Self-realization    123

42. The Time-bound Harvest: A Sonnet Of Effort And Reward    127

43. Passion's Reticence: A Sonnet On The Importance Of Prudent    130

Speech In Times Of Ire

44. The Vigilant's Discretion: A Sonnet On The Preservation Of    132

Friendships

45. Verbose Discretion: A Sonnet On The Importance Of Prudent    137

Speech

46. The Reticent's Caution: A Sonnet On The Power Of Words    138

47. Eloquent Reticence: A Sonnet On The Importance Of    139

Temperate Speech

48. The Pecuniary Privation: A Lesson In Lucidity And    141

Mindfulness

49. Champions Of Obscurity: A Sonnet Of Gratitude And    143

Remembrance

50. The Sonnet Of Penurious Peril    144

51. Tenacity Triumphant: A Sonnet Of Resolve And Persistence    146

52. Epistolary Ode To Valor And Amour    147

53. The Amorous Fervor: A Sonnet Of Passion And Tranquility    148

54. The Symphony Of Resilience: A Sonnet Of Lamentation And    151

Perseverance

55. Euphoric Adoration: A Sonnet Of Eternal Love    152

56. Empyreal Triumph: A Sonnet Of Inner Demons And Love's    155

Healing Power

57. The Luminous Horizon Of Hope    158

# Contents


58. The Enchained Heart's Lament     161

59. The Amorous Lunacy: A Sonnet Of Salvation And Poesy     162

60. The Enigma Of Self: A Ponderous Musing     163

61. The Fervent Attraction: A Sonnet Of Amorous Passion And Tranquility     164

62. The Beguiled Heart: A Sonnet On Love's Disappointment     166

63. The Enigmatic Harmony: A Sonnet Of Nongriat's Bifurcated Root Bridge     167

64. Umbrella Of Strength: A Sonnet On Facing Fears And Insecurities     168

65. Smit's Splendor: A Sonnet On The Intertwining Of Nature And Culture     169

66. The Posthumous Altruism Sonnet: "a Gift To Nature's Cycle"     170

67. Assertive Authenticity: A Sonnet Of Self-discovery     174

68. The Epiphany Of Lentils: A Sonnet Of Sovereignty     175

69. The Paradox Of Insanity: A Sonnet Of Sovereignty     177

70. Trials Triumphant: A Sonnet Of Fortitude And Resolution     178

71. Elysian Wanderings: A Sonnet To The Sylvan Glades     179

72. The Beauty Of Mohini     180

73. Logotherapy : A Sonnet     181

74. Lunaris Fortitudo     182

75. Cognitive Fortitude     183

76. Perdurable Mettle     184

77. Kudle Beach : A Sonnet     185

78. Pondicherry : A Sonnet     186

79. Tosh : A Sonnet     187

# Contents


80. Hampi : A Sonnet 188

Just For You 189

Note 195

# Foreword

Dear reader,

Welcome to the tenth installment of the Homo Sapiens series, "The Heart of Humanity: A Book of Eighty Poetic Meditations". In this work, Mawphniang Napoleon invites us to delve into the depths of humanity through a series of eighty thought-provoking poems. Each meditation explores various concepts and perspectives, including fortitude, resilience, sanguinity, fate, the meaning of life, and many others that are central to our understanding of who we are as human beings.

The poet's voice is both haunting and empowering, drawing us into a world of contemplation and reflection. Through their words, we are given the opportunity to contemplate the essence of our existence, to question our place in the world, and to find meaning in a world that often seems devoid of it.

This book is not just a collection of poems but a philosophical journey, one that invites us to think deeply about the complexities of being human. I encourage you to read this work with an open mind and heart, and to reflect upon the many insights and perspectives it offers. And I invite you to explore the other books in the Homo Sapiens series and other works by the same author, to continue your journey of self-discovery and understanding.

Sincerely,

A - Team

# Preface

This book, "Homo Sapiens Part-X," is a light,

That shines upon the Heart of Humanity,

It's pages etched with eighty poems so bright,

That delve into the depths of humanity.

The poet's pen, like a sword of truth,

Cuts through the haze to find what lies beneath,

The meaning of life, the nature of our youth,

And what it means to be human, in our wreath.

From fortitude to resilience, from fate

To sanguinity, each word is a reflection,

Of all that makes us human, of our state,

Of mind and soul, and the perfect connection.

So let us delve into this ocean deep,

Of understanding, where humanity can keep.

And find within these pages, a new view,

Of all the concepts that we often misconstrue.

For through the lens of poetry and rhyme,

We can see the world in a different light,

The struggles and triumphs, the love and the crime,

That shape the human experience, night after night.

So come, and let us journey to the core,

Of what it means to be human, evermore,

With open hearts and minds, let us explore,

The Heart of Humanity, in all its lore.

For this is a book that holds the key,

To understanding, to humanity.

Warm regards,

A - Team

# Acknowledgements

We acknowledge you, dear reader, yes you,
A lover of words, a seeker of truth,
A person who's searching for what is true
In this world of chaos and turmoil too.
You are here to read this book, it's true,
The tenth book in the Homo Sapiens series, it's new.
The Heart of Humanity, a book of eighty
Poetic meditations, a journey to see
What lies within us, our inner beauty
The core of our beings, so pure and so free
It delves into examination, a quest to be
Understood, a deep reflection of humanity.
From different perspectives, it tries to find
What makes us human, our hearts intertwined
With love and compassion, a feeling so kind
A thirst for knowledge, a search of the mind
This book explores it all, a journey of the blind
A path to enlightenment, a quest to be mankind.
Do read other books from the Homo Sapiens series,
An odyssey of words, a journey of tears
A quest to understand, a search for truth and clarity,
Discover the meaning of life, a journey to be free
The author, Mawphniang Napoleon, a poet's series
Of reflections, a journey of humanity's memories.
And don't forget, other books by the same author
A journey of words, a path to discover

ACKNOWLEDGEMENTS

The secrets of life, the wonders of the world

A quest for knowledge, a journey of discovery,

The author's voice, a guide to our story,

A journey to understand, a path to humanity.

We acknowledge you, dear reader, yes you

A seeker of truth, a lover of the truth

This book, The Heart of Humanity, is for you

A journey of reflection, a quest for the truth

A path to enlightenment, a journey to be free

In this world of chaos and turmoil, be humanity.

Warm regards,

A - Team

# Prologue

Verse 1:

We present to you, a book of reflection,

A journey into the heart of humanity,

Eighty poetic meditations, with intention

To delve into our understanding, with clarity.

From different perspectives, we'll explore our fate,

Our fortitude, resilience, and sanguinity.

Verse 2:

The poem on fortitude, a source of inspiration,

A measure of strength, that defines humanity,

A quality that helps us endure our situation,

And endure the hardships of life's reality.

It's what keeps us going, in the face of fate,

A symbol of resilience, and sanguinity.

Verse 3:

Resilience, a virtue, that's vital to our fate,

The ability to bounce back, with sanguinity,

It's what helps us overcome, our limitations,

And rise above the challenges of reality.

It's a testament to the strength of humanity,

And the power of our hearts, with clarity.

Verse 4:

Sanguinity, a state of mind, that brings clarity,

A positive outlook, that defies our fate,

It helps us find hope, in the face of adversity,

And maintain our spirit, with resilience and reality.

It's what gives us the strength, to face humanity,

And overcome the challenges, with fortitude.

Verse 5:

Our fate, a subject, that often clouds our clarity,

A mystery that has haunted humanity,

For centuries, we've struggled to understand,

Its purpose, and its meaning, with reality.

But with fortitude, resilience, and sanguinity,

We can face our fate, with confidence and clarity.

Verse 6:

The meaning of life, a subject of humanity,

A question that's plagued us, since the dawn of fate,

But with this book, we'll delve into its clarity,

And find answers, that will bring us reality.

With fortitude, resilience, and sanguinity,

We'll find our purpose, and the heart of humanity.

Envoi:

The heart of humanity, a source of clarity,

A journey that we undertake, with fate,

With fortitude, resilience, and sanguinity,

We'll find the answers, that bring us reality.

Do read other books, from the Homo Sapiens series,

And other books, by the same author, with clarity.

Warm regards,

A - Team

# 1. Retribution's Resolve: A Sonnet of Vindication

Oh sweet vindication, how oft thy flavor
Upon the palates of those who transgressed me initially,
And in my cerebral organ, thy acrid musings still manipulate
The injuries of the past, that still in me doth yearn.

But now, my epoch hath arrived, to compose a pericope
Inscribed with the ink of veracity, and not of mendacity,
A narrative of all the injustices that I did endure
At the hands of those who now with remorse doth ascend.

They perceived my reticence as a sign of frailty,
And so they inflicted the injuries that lacerated deeply,
But now they'll perceive, with each folio they shall peruse,
The fortitude that in my cardiac organ did ever reside.

So let them quiver at the prospect of perusal,
For in my verbiage, their faults shall be conspicuous.

For in my words, they'll find the truth they sought to hide,
And in my tale, their guilt shall be laid bare.

My silence was not weakness, but a strength inside,
A power that they could not understand or dare.

But now, with ink and paper in my hand,
I'll tell the story of the wrongs they've done,
And let the world know of their guilty stand,
And how they've lost, and I have won.

So let them tremble, let them shake with fear,
For in my words, their downfall is near.

And as they read the tales of their deceit,
They'll see that in my revenge, true victory is sweet.

And as they turn each page with trepidation,
They'll realize their own condemnation.

For in my words, they'll see their own reflection,
And in my tale, their own destruction.

And as they reach the final chapter,
They'll understand the true cost of their actions.

For my sweet revenge, it was not for pleasure,
But for the truth, and my own closure.

So let them read, and let them see,
The consequences of their deeds on me.

For in my words, they'll find the truth they sought to hide,
And in my tale, their guilt shall be laid bare.

And as they read the tales of their transgression,
They'll feel the weight of their own repression.

For in my words, they'll see the pain they've caused,
And in my tale, their own moral loss.

And as they reach the final verse,
They'll understand the true cost of their curse.

For my sweet revenge, it was not for malice,
But for the truth, and my own justice.

So let them read, and let them learn,
The consequences of their actions, in turn.

For in my words, they'll find the truth they sought to hide,
And in my tale, their guilt shall be laid bare.

And in my sweet revenge, true vindication will reside.

And as they finish reading my final lines,
They'll feel the weight of their own crimes.

For in my words, they'll see the harm they've done,
And in my tale, their own downfall begun.

And as they close the book, and look within,
They'll understand the true weight of their sin.

For my sweet revenge, it was not for glory,
But for the truth, and my own redemption story.

So let them read, and let them understand,
The consequences of their actions, and their reprimand.

For in my words, they'll find the truth they sought to hide,
And in my tale, their guilt shall be laid bare.

And in my sweet revenge, true justice will prevail.

And as they look upon the pages written,
They'll feel the weight of their own guilt smitten.

For in my words, they'll see the hurt they've caused,
And in my tale, their own moral loss.

And as they realize the truth I've spoken,
They'll understand the true weight of their token.

For my sweet revenge, it was not for victory,
But for the truth, and my own liberation story.

So let them read, and let them comprehend,
The consequences of their actions, until the end.

For in my words, they'll find the truth they sought to hide,
And in my tale, their guilt shall be laid bare.

And in my sweet revenge, true closure will reside.

# 2. The Paradox of Perfection: A Sonnet

The apogee of delusion is the belief that existence should be impeccable,
A fallacy oft perpetuated by the psyche;
For in the realm of mortal life, imperfection
Is but a natural state, a unique paradigm.

Luminescence and effulgence, oft coveted,
Are but ephemeral glimpses in a sea of misery;
And though we yearn for that which we extol,
We find that it doth come and swiftly depart.

Thus, let us not be beguiled by empty illusions,
Of flawless lives and eternal felicity;
For in this world of sorrow and vicissitudes,
Such notions are but phantasms of futility.

And though we may be assailed by doubts and anxieties,
We must remember that life's journey endures.

So let us not lament our foibles and blemishes,
But celebrate the beauty in our imperfections.

Let us embrace the notion that life
is a journey of learning, not a destination.

Let us realize that every obstacle, every failure,
every setback is a stepping stone
to our ultimate enlightenment.
Let us transcend the mundane and reach
for the sublime, for only then can we truly live.
Let us not be hindered by the illusion of perfection,
but strive for self-improvement, for the pursuit
of excellence is the ultimate goal.

Thus, let us be sagacious, evermore,
and in our quest for wisdom, let our hearts soar.

For in the grand scheme of things, our flaws and blemishes
Are but mere trifles, insignificant in the grand design;
For it is in our imperfections that we find our true selves,
And it is through our struggles that we truly refine.

Let us not be shackled by societal expectations,
But instead, let us forge our own path, with courage and conviction;
For true freedom lies in being true to ourselves,
And in embracing the unique beauty of our imperfection.

Let us not be afraid to make mistakes,
But instead, let us learn from them and grow;
For it is through our failures that we truly evolve,
And it is through our struggles that we truly know.

So let us not lament our flaws and blemishes,
But celebrate the beauty in our imperfections,

For in this realization, true wisdom blossoms,
And in its light, our souls truly find their afflictions.

Let us be sagacious, evermore,
And in our quest for wisdom, let our hearts soar.

# 3. Emancipation Through Torpor: A Sonnet of Alacrity and Tranquility

As portals open and the way is cleared,
With alacrity we break free from sloth,
The interval, though taxing, brought repose,
Preparing us for tasks that lie ahead.

Not punishment, but a chance to build and grow,
To strengthen heart, mind, and resolve, we strive,
To ready ourselves for journeys yet to know,
And face the world with renewed optimism.

Thus, let the portals open wide and true,
Through the gateway of the unknown we tread,
With valor and conviction, we pursue
The opportunities that lie ahead.

The interval was but a fleeting moment,
In the grand scheme, for greatness yet to come.

And so, with steadfast determination,
We forge ahead, undeterred by fear,
With eyes fixed firmly on our destination,
And hearts filled with the courage to persevere.

For though the road may be long and winding,
And obstacles may rise along the way,
We know that with each step we are binding
Ourselves to success, come what may.

So let us press on with undiminished zeal,
For greatness waits for those who dare to strive,
And in the end, it shall be our reward,
To bask in glory, and come alive.

For as the portals open, and we pass through,
We know that greatness is what we're due.

And so, with every step we take, we rise,
Elevated by our own perseverance,
For in the face of life's great unknowns, we prize
Our strength, our will, and our endurance.

For though the path ahead may be unclear,
And doubts may linger in our hearts and minds,
We trust in our abilities and cheer
For the victories yet to be defined.

So let us embrace the journey with grace,
And let our hearts be filled with hope and light,
For as we walk the path that lies ahead,
We know that greatness is always in sight.

And as the portals open wide, we see
The world before us, waiting for us to be.

And so, we march forth with purpose in our hearts,
Forging ahead with unwavering resolve,
For in this journey, we are but mere parts
Of a grand narrative that we must evolve.

We know that every step we take is crucial,
As we strive to reach our ultimate goal,
For in the end, it is not just the usual
Victory, but something much more whole.

We seek not fame, nor wealth, nor power,
But a sense of self, a feeling of true worth,
A sense of belonging, in this hour,
And a sense of purpose, that will birth.

So let us embrace the journey with grace,
For greatness awaits, as we find our place.

And as we journey on, we understand
That greatness is not just a destination,
But a journey in itself, a road to grand
Discovery, self-awareness, and revelation.

For in the struggles, we find our strength,
In the hardships, we find our will to survive,
And in the end, we find our true length

As we stand tall, and truly thrive.

So let us embrace the journey, not just the end,
For the journey is where we truly learn,
And as we journey on, we make amends
For the past, and for the future, we yearn.

For greatness is not just a destination,
But a journey that we must take with patience.

# 4. The Immeasurable Worth Sonnet

It doth not comport to quantify one's excellence
By the superficial approbation conferred;
For existence, in and of itself, possesses immeasurable value,
And deservability should not thus be undermined.

To evaluate oneself by the actions of others is futile,
Is to abdicate autonomy and dominance;
For value is not a metric of mere prosperity,
But an inherent virtue in one's essence.

Thus, let not the treatment of others serve as the yardstick,
By which one's value is computed and determined;
For true value resides within, not on the yardstick,
And should be cultivated and retained in contemplations.

Thus, let not the treatment of others serve as the key,
To unlocking the value within, release it.

And though the world may try to dim one's light,
With words of doubt and malice unrefined,
Do not let their perceptions be your plight,
For true worth lies within, not in their mind.

Let not the opinions of the many sway,

The path that you have chosen for yourself,
For true success is found in living true,
To the voice that speaks within, in your own wealth.

So let not others dictate your worth,
Or make you feel as though you're not enough,
For the measure of your value lies within,
And should be cherished, nurtured and loved.

And though the world may try to bring you low,
Remember your true worth and let it show.

And when the world seems harsh and unkind,
And doubts and fears within you start to climb,
Do not let their words and actions bind,
Your worth and value, they are not your kind.

For true worth is not found in outward show,
But in the strength and courage of one's soul,
And though the world may try to make you know,
You are not enough, let their words roll.

For you are more than what they can see,
More than their judgment and their pride,
You are a being of great complexity,
With worth and value that cannot be denied.

So let not others define your worth,
For true value lies within, let it burst forth.

And when the world around you starts to crumble,
Stand tall, for your worth is beyond measure, it is humble.

# 5. Ode to Erudite Consequentialism

Punditry of intellect, with perspicacity,
Discern the plethora of choices nigh,
And ponder each with a palpable acumen
Of worldly ramifications soaring high.

But those befuddled by dogmatism's creed,
Are myopic to the outcome's veracity,
And tether their thoughts in doctrine's chimera,
And principles of vacuous verity.

Thus let us endeavor to be sagacious,
And in our decisions, be consequential,
For wisdom's path, albeit arduous, is just,
And yields progression, whilst folly's leads to naught
But being engulfed in an abyssal darkness,
A life of vacuity, both paltry and fraught.

With lexicon rich and varied, let us weave
A tapestry of verse that's truly grand,
A hymn to wisdom, with our words conceive,
A symphony of thought, both bold and grand.

Let us not shy away from complexity,
But embrace it with aplomb and panache,

For in its depths, true beauty we'll discover,
And in its light, our minds will find their niche.

With eloquence, let us expound our thoughts,
And with our rhymes, create a melodious sound,
For in this sonnet, let us leave our mark,
And in its beauty, future generations will be astound.

So let us strive for greatness, evermore,
And in our verse, let our wisdom truly soar.

# 6. Ethereal Introspection

Though Oft we wander to distant lands,
In search of a happiness that's new,
But we forget that joy is found within,
In depths of self that we too often eschew.

Betwixt the self we were and self we're becoming,
We oft encounter strife and turmoil in our hearts,
In states of being we are loath to own,
And bile that from our every pore out starts.

We seek to purge our pasts of hours ill-spent,
To heal the wounds that time and fate have made,
But cure for souls that dying are, is lent,
In salves that to our wounded hearts are laid.

So let us strive to find the truest self,
And in that quest, true happiness will dwell,
For in the depths of our being, true wealth,
And the key to a life well-lived, we'll find as well.

And as we delve into the depths of our souls,
We'll find the answers to our deepest fears,
And in the quest for true self-control,
We'll shed the shackles of our past's tears.

For in the self, lies the power to heal,
And to find the peace that we so crave,
And as we come to truly know ourselves,
We'll find the strength to brave life's every wave.

So let us not in search of happiness,
Wander far and wide, but find it within,
For in the self, true joy and contentment is,
And in that quest, true purpose we'll begin.

And as we journey on, with hearts aglow,
Let us strive to find the truest self, and true happiness will follow.

And as we find the truest version of ourselves,
We'll discover the beauty in our imperfections,
For in embracing our humanity,
We'll find the strength to face life's tribulations.

For the quest for perfection is a futile chase,
And in its pursuit, true happiness is lost,
But in accepting ourselves, with grace,
We'll find the peace, at any cost.

And as we walk this path of self-discovery,
Let us not fear the unknown, but embrace it,
For in the depths of our souls, lies the key,
To true understanding and to transcend it.

So let us strive to find the truest self,

And in that quest, true happiness and inner peace we'll find, and nothing else.

# 7. Fortitude's Flight: A Sonnet of Solitude

In the secluded realm of introspection,
Where societal bonds are cast aside,
Lies the strength of conviction,
A steadfast compass, oft obscured by pride.

For within the tranquil confines of the mind,
The psyche flourishes, expands, and thrives,
In ways that cannot be when others bind,
And impede growth, to flourish and survive.

Therefore, let us not be swayed by those
Of weaker wills, but choose the path that's true,
With courage, audacity, and a steadfast nose,
For 'tis the noblest aspect of the few.

And let us rise above the fray, with strength unshaken,
A true and valorous path, unyielding, unbroken,
For in this solitude, one's virtue is awaken,
And fortitude, the key to life's unspoken.

And as we journey on this path alone,
Let us not fear the solitude, but embrace it,
For in this quietness, our souls have grown,
And found a depth of wisdom, unerased it.

For in the stillness of the mind, we find,
A clarity of thought, a steadfast guide,
That leads us to the truths that we must bind,
And to the self, we cannot help but abide.

And as we navigate this life's rough seas,
Let us not falter, but with strength press on,
For in this solitude, our souls will ease,
And find a peace, that in the world is gone.

So let us not be swayed by those who fear,
This path of solitude, but hold it dear.

And as we forge ahead, undeterred,
We'll shed the shackles of society,
And find within ourselves, a strength, unherd,
That will empower us to be free.

For in this solitude, we'll find a way,
To break the chains of conformity,
And rise above the fray, to pave our own way,
To true autonomy and liberty.

And as we tread this path, with heads held high,
We'll find our purpose and our destiny,
And with each step, we'll reach for the sky,
And find the courage to be truly free.

So let us not be swayed by fears or doubts,
But take the path of solitude, and find our way out.

And as we reach the summit of our quest,
We'll find the answers to our deepest doubts,
And with a sense of peace and inner rest,
We'll know that solitude was what it was about.

For in this solitude, we've come to know,
The truth about ourselves and our desires,
And with a newfound strength and inner glow,
We'll set our souls on fire.

So let us not be swayed by those who mock,
This path of solitude, that we have chosen,
For in this path, we've unlocked,
The power to be truly self-frozen.

And as we journey on, with hearts aglow,
We'll find the strength to face any kind of woe.

# 8. Eternal Embrace: A Sonnet of Undying Love

Entwined in passionate adulation,
A love that's pure, yet fiercely ardent,
With boundless devotion, our souls do blend,
As each to the other clings and doth extend.
Through tempests fierce and challenges severe,
In one another, strength and solace find,
With steadfast trust and faith, we persevere,
To weather every storm and peace unbind.
In giving, receiving, cherishing,
We learn to love in all its boundless expanse,
With purpose true and joy forever relishing,
In love, our truest selves do we enhance.
Two hearts, two souls, united as one,
With passion deep, undivided, and ever-won.
And as we navigate this life's rough seas,
In love, we find a safe haven, and true ease.

And as we journey through this life, with love,
We'll find the strength to face any kind of woe,
For in the depths of our hearts, we'll find a dove,
That guides us through the storms and makes us whole.

For love is not just a feeling or a thought,
But a force that shapes our very being,

It's the light that guides us out of the dark,
And the peace that brings us a sense of freeing.

And as we walk this path of life, together,
Let us not fear the unknown, but embrace it,
For in love, we'll find the strength to weather,
Any storm, and in it, we'll transcend it.

So let us entwine our souls in love,
And in that bond, true joy and purpose we'll find, and nothing above.

And as we stand at life's crossroads,
With love as our guide, we'll make our choice,
For in its light, we'll see the true roads,
And the path to our truest voice.

For love is not just a fleeting feeling,
But a force that shapes our very destiny,
It's the light that guides us through the healing,
And the peace that brings us tranquility.

And as we walk this path of life, hand in hand,
Let us not falter, but with strength press on,
For in love, we'll find the courage to stand,
And the hope to face the unknown.

So let us entwine our souls in love,
And in that bond, true strength and purpose we'll find, and nothing
above.

# 9. The Neoplasm of the Cerebrum: A Cycle of Desolation and Lamentations

My cerebrum, the wellspring and epicenter of my mortal span,
A breeding ground for maladies and lamentations,
A bastille where my very essence abides,
Imprisoned in a cycle of desolation and lamentations.

For just as in the corpus, ailment may disseminate,
And ravage all that's immaculate and veracious and beneficent,
So too within my cerebrum, a neoplasm propagates,
Devouring all that once was comprehended.

And though I endeavor to keep my cerebrum in repose,
To safeguard against the somber and negative,
The acrimonious verity persists, that all ailment
Is but a symptom of a more profound quandary.

For in my cerebrum, my essence finds its wellspring,
And there my very existence takes its trajectory,
A cycle of desolation and resignation without expiation.

But still, I strive to break this cycle,
To transcend the maladies and lamentations,
And find solace in the light, that is my mind,

For in it, my true self, awaits liberation.

For in this quest, I find my purpose,
To unlock the mysteries of my cerebrum,
And in this, I find my true worth,
For in this quest, my mind, becomes my kingdom.

And though the journey may be arduous,
With obstacles and challenges to overcome,
I know that in my cerebrum, there is a spark,
That will guide me to the light, and the end of this gloom.

For in the quest for self-discovery,
I must delve deep into my mind,
And confront the demons and insecurities,
That have been holding me back, all this time.

But with each step, I gain new insight,
And understanding of my very essence,
And in this, I find my true might,
To transcend my cerebral maladies, with persistence.

For my cerebrum, is not just a bastille,
But a gateway to true understanding,
And in this quest, I find true liberation,
And the power to transcend, my own suffering.

Thus, I shall not be defeated by maladies,
That may arise in the sanctum of my cerebrum,

For in the quest for self-discovery, I shall rise,
And transcend the lamentations, that may come.

For I know that within my cerebrum, lies
The key to unlock my full potential,
And in this quest, I shall find my prize,
A true understanding of my essential.

So let me not be held captive,
By the maladies that may assail,
For in the quest for self-discovery, I shall thrive,
And transcend the limitations, that may veil.

For in my cerebrum, there is a light,
That will guide me to true understanding,
And in this quest, I shall find my might,
To transcend the maladies, and find true standing.

And as I journey on this path,
Of self-discovery and transcendence,
I know that in my cerebrum, the aftermath,
Will be a true understanding of my existence.

For in this quest, I shall find my true self,
And the purpose that I was meant to fulfill,
And in this, I shall find my true wealth,
A true understanding of my cerebrum's will.

And though the journey may be long,

And the path may be difficult to tread,
I know that in my cerebrum, there is a song,
That will guide me, till the end.

So let me not be held captive,
By the maladies that may assail,
For in the quest for self-discovery, I shall strive,
And transcend the limitations, that may veil.

# 10. Nefelibata: A Sonnet of Fantasia and Longing

I, a denizen of nebulous cogitations,
Wherein my encephalon doth depict a more opulent hue
Of moments that irradiate with refulgent scintillations,
And azure vistas aglow with tints of auric and cerulean.

A utopia of my own imagination,
Where cumuli of apprehensions and phobias do dissipate
And all is tranquility and suave equanimity
As I ruminate the sunset's melodious strophe.

But alas, my feet have yet to tread its terra firma
For though I've fantasized of this fair Arcadia
I've not yet uncovered the means to reach its boundaries
And thus, my heart remains in profound lamentations.

I, a sojourner in the realm of musings,
Wherein my intellect doth depict a vista grand,
Of moments that radiate with effulgent gleamings,
And azure horizons aglow with tints of gold and cerulean.

A utopia of my own fancy,
Where cumuli of anxieties and terrors do dissipate
And all is serenity and suave placidity
As I contemplate the sunset's melodious canto.

But alas, my soles have yet to tread its soil
For though I've fantasized of this fair Arcadia
I've not yet discovered the means to reach its bounds
And thus, my heart remains in profound lamentations.

Though oft beset by doubts and fears untold,
I still embrace the hope that guides my way,
Towards that ethereal dune, where dreams take hold,
And I, with heart and soul, may find my way.

For hope, in its eternal, shining light,
Doth guide my footsteps through the darkest night,
And lends a strength, that in my heart doth fight
Against the doubts, that seek to steal my sight.

For hope is not a thing, that can be bought,
But something that within our souls doth dwell,
A spark, that in the darkest hour, is sought,
And kindles into flame, a story to tell.

So I, with hope as my companion, tread
Towards that ethereal dune, where all is shed
And I, in freedom's light, am truly led
To find my path, that I may be unbound

And in that place, where dreams take shape, I'll find
My purpose and my peace, that I may bind
My heart and soul, to that which is divine

And there, in glory, my journey will entwine

With fate's design, and I, in harmony
Shall live, in that ethereal dune, forever free.

Upon the vista of each passing day,
I tread with cautious step, towards that clime,
Wherein my heart and soul doth find its way
To realms of utmost joy, in perfect rhyme.

Forsooth, my journey's end, though far off yet,
Is but the culmination of my quest,
Wherein my heart, with freedom's banner met,
Shall beat in harmony, forever blessed.

A utopia, a land of pure desire,
Where all my hopes and dreams shall be fulfilled,
And I, with heart and mind, shall upward soar,
With naught to hinder me, nor doubts to stilled.

For there, my heart shall be forever free,
In that fair land, my soul shall find its destiny.

# 11. The Paradox of Fortitude: A Maleficent Conundrum

The fortitude of one oft proves maleficent,

For whilst others necessitate aid to survive,

One's ever willing to proffer solace, hence

Yet when in need themselves, scarce help's alive.


They find a single individual willing

To proffer a shoulder for leaning upon,

For they deem their own strength inadequate

And themselves too humble to sustain one.


But to be truly fulfilled, one must learn to rely

On one's own inner strength and resilience,

And not seek validation from others, high and dry.


For true strength lies not in self-aggrandizement,

But in the ability to stand tall,

In the face of adversity, with humility and persistence.


And as we journey through life, with courage,

Let us not seek validation from others,

But find it within ourselves, and with humility, we will find solace.


For the path to true self-actualization,

Is through the cultivation of self-reliance,

And the rejection of societal validation.

For only by embracing our own limitations,
Can we transcend them, and attain true strength,
And in humility, find true satisfaction.

Thus, let us reject the superficial,
And strive for a deeper understanding,
Of the human condition, and our own purpose.

For it is in this quest for self-knowledge,
That we find true fulfillment, and inner peace,
And the fortitude to face life's challenges.

Thus, let us embrace our own humility,
And in so doing, find true strength and solace,
As we journey through this mortal reality.

And as we journey on, let us not forget
The importance of empathy and compassion,
For it is in understanding others, that we truly connect.

Let us strive to see the world through others' eyes,
And to walk in their shoes, with empathy and grace,
For it is through this understanding, that true wisdom lies.

And in this wisdom, we find true strength and fortitude,
For it allows us to navigate life's storms with ease,
And to rise above our own limitations, with gratitude.

So let us embrace humility and self-reliance,
And let us strive for empathy and understanding,
For in these virtues, true strength and solace will abide.

And as we navigate this mortal reality,
Let us find solace in our own inner strength and humility,
And in so doing, attain true fulfillment and serenity.

And as we go forth, let us not forget
The importance of self-reflection and introspection,
For it is in understanding ourselves, that we truly connect.

Let us take the time to delve deep within,
To explore our thoughts, emotions and desires,
For it is through this self-exploration that true growth begins.

And in this growth, we find true strength and fortitude,
For it allows us to navigate life's twists and turns with grace,
And to rise above our own limitations, with gratitude.

So let us embrace humility and self-reliance,
And let us strive for self-knowledge and understanding,
For in these virtues, true strength and solace will abide.

And as we navigate this mortal reality,
Let us find solace in our own inner strength and humility,
And in so doing, attain true fulfillment and serenity.

For it is through the cultivation of these virtues,

That we find true purpose, and live a life of meaning,

And in so doing, we achieve true transcendence.

# 12. The Resilience of Kongthei: A Tale of Woe and Fortitude

Oh hapless Kongthei, in the environs of Mumbai's streets doth reside
Beset by dire necessitation to earn sustenance for her progeny
The sole means by which she can evade financial quagmire
Is through the sale of carnal favors, a path most ignoble and unsavory.

Her kith and kin with acrimony and opprobrium are filled,
Towards her vocation, yet despite the constant tribulation,
And abuse she endures in pursuit thereof, alternative is nought,
Thus, she must persist in her endeavors, toil, and affliction.

But in the face of such dire straits and utter destitution,
Kongthei's resilience and determination, doth shine with great illumination,
For in the face of adversity, she rises with great fortitude,
To provide for her progeny, with great fortitude and fortitude.

Her existence, a constant battle against societal disdain
And the perils of her profession, a never-ending chain
But in her struggle, one finds a strength most admirable
A will to survive, in the face of poverty, most admirable.

Kongthei's plight, a reflection of societal ills

A system that breeds poverty, and the oppressed it kills
But in the face of such dire straits and utter destitution,
Kongthei's resilience and determination, doth shine with great illumination.

But despite her struggles, Kongthei remains unbroken
For within her, there burns a fierce determination, unspoken
A will to survive, to provide for her progeny
And to rise above the societal ills that hinder her destiny.

Her spirit, like a phoenix, rises from the ashes
To face each day with courage and unshakable resolves
For though her path may be marred by societal clashes
She persists, with an indomitable spirit that evolves.

For though she may be maligned by those who cannot see
The strength and determination within her, that sets her free
She knows that in her heart, she is a warrior, unyielding
Fighting for her survival, in a world that is unyielding.

And in the face of all the struggles that she must bear
Kongthei's spirit shines, like a beacon, bright and fair
A symbol of hope, for those who are downtrodden
And a reminder that in the face of adversity, one can rise, unbroken.

But alas, her journey is not one without its cost
For in the pursuit of survival, her humanity is lost
Her innocence and dignity, sacrificed in the name of survival
And her soul, forever scarred by the harshness of life's survival.

Kongthei's story, a reflection of a society's failure
To provide for its citizens, and to lift them from their direness
It is a story of a woman who was forced to sell her labor
To escape the perils of poverty, in a world that is heartless.

But despite it all, Kongthei remains unbroken
For within her, there burns a fierce determination, unspoken
A will to survive, to provide for her progeny
And to rise above the societal ills that hinder her destiny.

And though her path may be filled with struggles, and strife
She persists, with an indomitable spirit, that continues to thrive.
A warrior, unyielding, in a world that is unyielding.
And a reminder that in the face of adversity, one can rise, unbroken.

# 13. Nalagon of Ataraxia: A Sonnet of Longing and Serenity

Oh pensive spirit, how doth thy psyche yearn
To traverse realms obscure, where eudaimonia reigns
And contemplations serene, like zephyrs, ethereal burn
To assuage the intellect and dispel all its pains.

Ataraxia, a bastion of equanimity
A sanctuary of repose, where anxieties abate
A place where I, in exquisite serenity,
May attain deliverance from all my psyche's afflictions.

But alas, my soles have yet to tread its terra firma
For though I've heard tell of this idyllic utopia
I've not yet discovered the means to reach its firmament
And thus, my spirit remains in melancholic melancholia.

But still, I'll cherish hope, that one day anon
I'll find my way to ataraxia's strand.

Oh weary soul, how doth thy essence long
To find a haven, free from worldly woes
A realm of serenity, where peace and calm belong
And in its embrace, new life, one finds to compose.

I'll meander through verdant fields of green
And immerse in rivulets of tranquility
My mind and body, in serenity, will be seen
And bask in the repose of equanimity.

I'll let the gentle zephyrs, so pure and sweet
Caress my visage and still my tumultuous thoughts
And in this haven of peace, my mind shall meet
With sagacity and my soul, with healing brought.

For in ataraxia's domain, I'll find my home
And there, my spirit, forever, shall roam.

# 14. Melancholy's Haven: A Sonnet of Domiciliary Disquietude

Upon returning home, where many find cheer,
I find instead a sense of fear and dread,
For in my domicile, so fraught with care,
I find my shoulders burdened, bowed, and led
To bear the weight of duties left unmet,
And issues plaguing all within its walls.
My heart is heavy with the thought, and yet
I cannot shake this feeling's downward falls.

The weight of familial obligations
And the unresolved conflicts that linger
Are a constant reminder of my limitations
And the extent of my emotional suffering.
And yet, I cannot help but feel trapped
In this cycle of misery, with no escape.

But I remind myself that true liberation
Is not just about being free from my home's constraints
But about overcoming the challenges
That come with it and finding inner peace.

For it is in the face of adversity,

That we truly test our mettle and find
The strength to rise above our fears and doubts
And find the courage to face whatever comes our way.

And so, I will strive to find solace
In the midst of my domestic turmoil,
And find true liberation and peace
In the face of my familial obligations.

For in the end, it is not the place
But the person we become that truly matters,
And I will emerge victorious,
Having found true liberation and peace,
In the midst of my domestic turmoil.

And so, I will continue to strive
To find inner peace and tranquility
In the midst of my domestic turmoil,
Through introspection, self-reflection and mindfulness
And in doing so, I will come to understand
That true liberation is not just about being free
From the constraints of our surroundings,
But about finding inner freedom and peace within ourselves.

For it is in the face of adversity
That we truly test our mettle,
And find out who we truly are,
And what we are truly capable of.

And so, I will embrace the challenges
That come with my home, and face them head-on,
Knowing that in doing so,
I will find true liberation and peace.

For it is through facing our fears,
And overcoming our doubts,
That we truly find the strength
To rise above our limitations,
And find true liberation and peace,
In the midst of our domestic turmoil.

So, I will continue to strive,
With steadfast determination and fortitude,
To find true liberation and peace,
In the midst of my domestic turmoil.

# 15. Exaltation's Egress: A Sonnet of Domestic Turmoil

With exaltation, multitudes egress
But I, with consternation, cannot do so
For mine abode is fraught with anarchy and distress
And altercation, betwixt parentals doth flow

Despite my endeavors to pacify and alleviate
Myself, vexation still doth ensnare me fast
For domicile, a haven, doth now belie
And leave me with a sensation of horror aghast

Thus, I am ensnared in this plight of misery
Wherein my bosom doth ache and psyche doth fret
For home, once sanctuary, doth now manifest
Itself as the origin of discord and regret

The domestic strife that consumes my life
Is a test of fate that I must endure
For only through this turmoil and strife
Can I hope to find true liberation

But still, I hold on to hope, and strive
To attain that elusive tranquility.

With steadfast determination and fortitude

I will rise above this domestic anarchy
And find the peace and serenity
That I so desperately seek.

For though my home may be a source of pain
It is also the place where I must remain
To confront and overcome the turmoil
That threatens to consume my very soul.

And in the end, I know that I will emerge
Victorious, having conquered the chaos
And found true liberation and peace
In the midst of my domestic turmoil.

And as I navigate this tempestuous sea
Of domestic strife, I remind myself
That true liberation is not just about being free
From the shackles of our surroundings, but about
Overcoming the challenges that life presents
And emerging stronger and more resilient

For it is in the face of adversity
That we truly test our mettle,
And find out who we truly are.

And so, I will continue to strive
To find peace and tranquility within myself
And in my home, knowing that true liberation
Is a journey, not a destination.

For in this journey, I will find my strength
And the courage to face whatever challenges
Life may throw my way.

And in the end, I will emerge victorious,
Having found true liberation and peace,
In the midst of my domestic turmoil.

# 16. Sanguineous Sufferance: A Sonnet of Phobia

The angst of existence doth oft assail my psyche,
A neurosis born of blood that doth appear
In nausea and excrement, a harsh plight
That doth my very being now endear.

The weight of being doth oppress my soul,
A yoke that doth nought but misery bring.
With every passing day, my will doth cower,
No end to this haemorrhagic suffering.

But still, I'll strive to bear this load with stoicism,
And seek a cure for this malady of the flesh.
Though life may oft be harsh and harsh to bear,
I'll persevere in search for a higher truth.

So let me bear this yoke with Nietzschean fortitude,
And find solace in the eternal recurrence.
For in this cycle of suffering and rebirth,
I'll transcend the human condition, and reach a state of amor fati.

And in this transcendence, I'll find my will to power,
A drive to overcome the limitations of the self.
For in embracing the eternal recurrence,
I'll find true freedom, and a state of self-overcoming.

But not all may see the value in this struggle,
For some may cling to comfortable delusions.
But I, with eyes wide open, will not muffle
The call of the eternal recurrence's conclusions.

For in this cycle of life and death we find,
The ultimate meaning of our being and our mind.
And in embracing it, we transcend the mortal coil,
And find our place in the eternal recurrence's toil.

So let us not fear the fear of life, my friends,
But embrace it with open hearts, until the very end.

For in this embrace, we'll find our true selves,
And transcend the mortal bounds of human delves.

We'll rise above the petty fears and doubts,
And find our strength in the eternal cycle's routs.

For in the end, it is not death we should fear,
But a life lived in ignorance and without cheer.

So let us embrace the eternal recurrence,
And find our true selves in its grand occurrence.

For in its infinite loops and endless turns,
We'll find our purpose, and our true selves will burn.

And in this burning, we'll transcend our mortal state,
And find eternal peace in the eternal fate.


So let us embrace the eternal recurrence,
And find our true selves in its grand occurrence.

# 17. Nasal Nemesis: A Sonnet of Suffering

The maladies of life oft assail my mind,
A weight that bears upon my well-being,
A trial that my health doth oft assail,
And leaves me to partake in bitter draught of life,
A chalice of woe that my soul doth bewail.

The rhinorrhea that doth my nose assail,
A host of woes that steals the breath of life,
It saps my strength and leaves me weak and frail,
And steals the joy of life with every sniff.

But still, I'll strive to bear this load with grace,
And find a way to rise above the pain.
For though the path is steep and hard to face,
I'll hope for health and joy to come again.

Thus, let me take this bitter cup with pride,
And find the fortitude to make my soul abide,
For though the trials of life may oft assail,
My will to endure shall ever remain.

And in the end, when my life doth wane,
I'll look back on these trials with disdain,
For in their midst, my strength and will were gained,

And in their wake, my soul did ever abide.

And though the road ahead may be uncertain,
And though the darkness may seem to prevail,
I'll hold fast to the light of hope within,
And never let despair my spirit assail.

For every step I take, I'll take with pride,
And in each step, my strength will be multiplied,
And in the end, I'll rise up to the sky,
With head held high, and victorious cry.

And though the journey may be long and hard,
And though the path may be beset with woes,
I'll tread it with steadfast heart and guard,
And in the end, I'll find my peace and repose.

For in the end, it's not the destination,
But the journey that shapes our souls and nation.

# 18. The Paradox of Shylock: A Test of Kismet

In the annals of venal history,
My name shall forever be inscribed
As the avaricious Shylock of Venice,
Whose insatiable greed was maligned
By the pen of Shakespeare, in his play
The Merchant of Venice. Though I won
A defamation case against the bard,
The victory was but a pyrrhic one,
For I was left with but a pittance of gold,
Compared to the wealth that he had garnered
From his portrayal of me.

But my woes did not end there, for I found
Myself mired in debt, unable to pay
The loans I had taken for my chariots
And for the purchase of unicorns,
Before the Black Death wrought its destruction.
My financier, Aunty Ropsy and her nephew,
William, who had been a friend and brother,
Now look upon me with disdain and hatred.

In my youth, I was ignorant of the fact
That my mother had availed herself of loans,
And left them to me upon her decease.

But now, with the weight of debt upon me,
I must toil without respite, and sacrifice
My youthful days, in order to attain
Liberation from the shackles of debt.

And yet, as I ponder on the cost
Of this sacrifice, I cannot help but feel
A sense of dismay, for in my quest
For freedom and success, I fear I'll lose
The joy and happiness that youth and carefree days
Can bring to one, and end up empty, hollow, and undone.

Thus, I must weigh the cost, and choose my path,
For in this game, there's no going back.
To sacrifice or not, that is the question,
That only time and fate can provide an answer.

But as I tread this path, I cannot help
But feel a sense of bitterness and regret,
For the loss of my youth, and the toll
That this quest for financial stability
Has taken on my mental and emotional well-being.
I find myself plagued by insecurity,
Paranoia, and depression, which are hard
To explain or handle, especially at a young age.

But in the end, I know that I must press on,
For there is no other choice but to strive
Towards the goal of liberation, and to never

Allow myself to be defeated by the trials
That life has thrown at me. I must remain steadfast,
And never give up, no matter how great
The obstacles that may come my way.

For in the end, it is not the gold or wealth
That truly matters, but the strength of will
And character that one possesses,
To rise above adversity and to triumph
In the face of hardship and defeat.

And so, I shall continue to strive
Towards my goal, with cand verity,
For I am Shylock of Venice, and I will not be defeated.

And though my name may forever be tarnished
By the accusations of greed and avarice,
I will not let it define me or control
My actions. For I am more than just a label
That others have placed upon me. I am a man
With my own dreams, aspirations and ambition
And I will fight to make them a reality.

I will work tirelessly, day and night
To earn my wealth, and to pay back my debts
With interest, to those who have loaned me.
I will not rest until I have achieved
Financial stability, and have regained
The respect and trust of those who have doubted me.

And once I have accomplished this, I will use
My newfound wealth and influence, to help
Those who are less fortunate, and to give back
To the community that has given me so much.

For in the end, it is not the gold or wealth
That truly matters, but the way we use it
To make the world a better place for all.

And so, I will continue on my journey
With cand verity, and a steadfast heart
For I am Shylock of Venice, and I will not be defeated.

But as I strive towards my goals, I cannot forget
The bitter lessons that life has taught me.
I have learned that greed and avarice
Are not the path to true happiness,
And that there is more to life than just wealth and fame.

I have come to understand the importance
Of humility, kindness, and generosity.
I have come to realize that true success
Is not measured by the amount of gold
One possesses, but by the love and respect
Of those around us, and by the good
That we do in the world.

And so, as I continue on my journey,

I will strive to be a better man,
To be kind and compassionate,
And to use my wealth and influence
For the betterment of all.

I will not let my past mistakes
Define me or control me,
For I am Shylock of Venice,
And I will not be defeated.

I will rise above my past,
And create a brighter future
For myself and for those around me.
For in the end, it is not the gold or wealth
That truly matters, but the person we become.

# 19. Quantum Conundrum: A Mind's Befuddlement

Phenomenological quandary, perplexing plight
Quantum mechanics, a mind's obfuscation
My intellect in shambles, left bewildered
Conceptual paradoxes, my brain embroiled

Spatial wave-particle dichotomy, a plight
Uncertainty principle, a constant affliction
Incoherent notions, left me perplexed
In a state of cognitive dissonance, vexed

But through the chaos, a glimmer of solace
For in the subatomic realm, all may reconcile
With the mysteries of the quantum sphere
And unlock the secrets held so dear

Thus, though my mind may be in disarray
I shall persevere, unravel this complexity
With stoic fortitude and philosophical grace
In the quest for truth, I shall not falter, nor trace

And with each unraveled mystery, I'll find
A deeper understanding of the cosmic mind.

And so I delve into the abyss of thought

With epistemological fervor, I'm fraught
The ontological questions, I must explore
To unlock the secrets of the quantum core

The Heisenberg principle, a confounding curse
But also a key to unlock the universe
The wave-function collapse, a mystery untold
But with each breakthrough, a story to be told

My mind in a state of superposition
As I navigate the realms of cognition
In search of the ultimate unification
Of the micro and macrocosm, a fusion

And though the journey may be long and arduous
I shall not falter, for the truth is auspicious
In the end, the answers we shall find
In the quantum realm, the truth is one of a kind.

And as I journey through the realms of physics
I'm faced with the ultimate ontological crisis
The question of reality, what does it mean?
Is it a mere construct or truly seen?

The Copenhagen interpretation, a guide
But also a source of confusion and divide
The many-worlds theory, a mind-bending thought
But also a possibility, to be sought

And so I ponder and I contemplate
The nature of existence, it's state
Is reality just a perception
Or is it something with a true dimension

The mysteries of the quantum world
Leave my mind in a state of unfurled
But I shall not give up on this quest
For the truth, it is what I manifest

And with each step, I'll come to know
The secrets of the universe, to show.

As I delve deeper into this abyss
I find myself in a state of bliss
For in the quest for truth and understanding
I find a sense of purpose, expanding

The concept of entanglement, a wonder
A connection between all, a thunder
The non-locality of quantum states
A realization that leaves me in a daze

The Bell's theorem, a test of fate
A challenge to our reality's state
But with each discovery, a new light
A path towards understanding, in sight

And so I continue on this journey

With a sense of purpose, not in a hurry
For the truth is not a destination
But a journey of self-realization

And as I unlock the secrets of the mind
I find myself in a state of cosmic bind
A connection to the universe, divine
A realization, that I am entwined.

And as I unravel the mysteries of the quantum realm,
I find myself in a state of transcendence, overwhelmed
The concept of observer effect, a revelation
A reminder that our perception shapes the equation.

The Schrodinger's cat, a paradoxical quandary
A reminder of the duality, it's a scary
The collapse of the wave function, a conundrum
But also a key to unlock the secrets, a sum of

And so I delve deeper into the abyss
With an open mind, I cannot miss
The beauty of the quantum realm, it's a treasure
A source of inspiration, beyond measure

And as I unlock the secrets of the universe
I find myself in a state of cosmic terse
A connection to the all, a realization
A reminder that we are part of the equation

And so I continue on this journey
With a sense of purpose, not in a hurry
For the truth is not a destination
But a journey of self-realization, a sensation.

As I traverse the realms of quantum physics,
I find myself in a state of metaphysical bliss,
The concept of non-duality, a profound realization,
A reminder that everything is interconnected, a sensation.

The principle of complementarity, a conundrum,
A reminder that duality is just an assumption,
The concept of observer effect, a revelation,
A reminder that our perception shapes reality, a sensation.

And so I delve deeper into the abyss,
With an open mind, I cannot miss,
The beauty of the quantum realm, it's a treasure,
A source of inspiration, beyond measure.

And as I unlock the secrets of the universe,
I find myself in a state of cosmic verse,
A connection to the all, a realization,
A reminder that we are part of the equation, a sensation.

And so I continue on this journey,
With a sense of purpose, not in a hurry,
For the truth is not a destination,
But a journey of self-realization, a sensation.

As I delve deeper into the quantum realm,
I find myself in a state of cosmic helm,
The concept of quantum entanglement, a marvel,
A reminder that everything is connected, a travel.

The concept of quantum superposition, a wonder,
A reminder that reality is not asunder,
The principle of quantum decoherence, a conundrum,
A reminder that the quantum realm is not a kingdom.

The concept of quantum teleportation, a mystery,
A reminder that the quantum realm is not a history,
The principle of quantum nonlocality, a realization,
A reminder that the quantum realm is beyond visualization.

As I delve deeper into the quantum realm,
I find myself in a state of cosmic helm,
The concept of quantum decoherence, a conundrum,
A reminder that the quantum world is not always serene.

The principle of quantum tunneling, a wonder
A reminder that reality is not always under
The concept of quantum coherence, a marvel
A reminder that the quantum world is not always aravel

And so I continue on this journey
With a sense of purpose, not in a hurry
For the truth is not a destination

But a journey of self-realization, a sensation

The concept of quantum computing, a mystery
A reminder that the quantum world is not always history
The principle of quantum cryptography, a realization
A reminder that the quantum world is beyond visualization

And as I unlock the secrets of the universe
I find myself in a state of cosmic verse
A connection to the all, a realization
A reminder that we are part of the equation, a sensation.

# 20. Perambulating Paddies: A Sonnet of Syadheh

Perambulating through the verdant paddies of Syadheh, my idyllic hamlet,
I immerse my pedes in the crystalline Umtrew,
Which courses through the sylvan valley,
Beneath the majestic peaks of Lum Sohpetbneng.

The zephyrs fill the air with their melody,
As the fronds dance in the autumnal breeze,
And the panoply of hues they display
Are a feast for the eyes in fleeting glimpses.

But the barren, arid spots of sandy gravel,
Glisten only in the occasional beam of sunlight,
Which serves only to accentuate their desolation.

The avian inhabitants, wisely, abstain
From song, for there is naught but thorny locusts,
And the forest's edge is far beyond their reach.

As I traverse the barren, human-trodden path
Towards the summit of Lum Sohpetbneng,
I am assailed by memories of days gone by;
Of young lads playing with their phones and tending their herds,
Of Rana Kharkongor's melodious strains

Emanating from a rusted, ancient Walkman.

Fishermen cast their lines with focused intent,
Hoping to reap a bountiful harvest
Before nightfall, to provide for their kin.

And the great black serpent stalks its rodent prey,
As this place, steeped in the stories of many,
Is a realm of contentment for those who visit.

But as I turn to depart, I am beset
With a sense of existential dread,
For in this land of beauty, I am yet
A stranger, my path yet unled.

For though I've wandered through this verdant land,
And bathed in the Umtrew's crystal strand,
I am but a transient, passing through,
With nary a mark upon this land to do.

And as I gaze upon the Lum Sohpetbneng,
I am humbled by its grandeur, and its strength,
For though my time here may be fleeting,
Its legacy shall endure at great length.

And so, I take my leave, with heart full of awe,
And with a sense of reverence, and a touch of raw,
For though my journey here may be at an end,
The memories of this land, shall remain my friend.

And as I journey forth, my thoughts do dwell
On the beauty and the solitude of this land,
And the stories etched in each pebble and shell,
That are woven in the fabric of this grand

And though my steps may take me far away,
And though my path may lead me to new lands,
The memories of Syadheh shall forever stay,
Etched in my heart, with loving hands.

For in this land, I found a sense of peace,
A sense of belonging, that I did not know existed,
And though my journey may never cease,
I shall forever carry Syadheh in my breast.

And as I wander through life's winding paths,
I shall remember the Umtrew's flowing rhapsody,
And the grandeur of the Lum Sohpetbneng,
And the beauty of Syadheh's serenity.

And though my steps may take me far away,
And though my path may lead me to new lands,
The memories of Syadheh shall forever stay,
Etched in my heart, with loving hands.

# 21. Christine de Pisan: The Trailblazer of Women's Literature in Medieval Europe

In days of yore, when chivalry did reign,

And damsels fair did grace the royal hall,

A progeny was born, of noble, learned strain,

Whose sire, Tommaso, did hold high thrall

With Charles the Fifth, renowned astronomer,

And thus, this offspring, Christine de Pisan, hight,

Was gifted with an erudition rare,

And swiftly proved her acumen and insight.

Verily, she penned such poesy sublime,

That even in her tendril youth, it shone,

But alas, in those days, 'twas not in time

For womankind to pursue such arts alone.

Matrimony came, and progeny, but when fate

Took both her sire and her spouse, she did not vacillate,

But instead, turned to her quill with zeal,

And soon, her oeuvre did patrons' hearts steal.

Monarchs, queens, and lords did offer aid and wealth,

And Christine de Pisan's fame did spread by stealth.

She wrote of women's rights with fervor bold,

And even Joan of Arc, did she extol.

Though death did come in 1430, her story
Lives on, as first true female scribe in glory.

And thus, her legacy did endure
Through time and tide, her works still read and pure,
A luminary in a world of men
Where women's voices oft went unheard or dimmed.
Christine de Pisan, a trailblazer true,
Who shattered the mold and dared to see it through.
A shining exemplar of what one can do
When passion burns and talent shines anew.
Her name, a symbol of strength and grace,
A reminder of what we can achieve
When we dare to break free from society's pace
And follow our own hearts, and our own beliefs.
So let us honor her, this poet fair
And pledge to keep her legacy alive, with care.

Her verse and prose, a testament to skill,
A legacy that will forever thrill,
A woman ahead of her time, a force
Who broke the chains and took a different course.
Her words, a symphony of rhyme and thought,
A celebration of women, oft unsought.
Her message, clear and true, a clarion call
For all to rise and break away from thrall.
She stood for what she believed and fought
For equality and women's rights, a sought
After voice In a world that was unjust

But through her words, she shone, a beacon of trust.
Christine de Pisan, a name to remember,
A woman who, in her time, did truly render
A change in the world, and set a new standard,
For all women to follow, and to ponder.

But her legacy is not just confined
To the past, her message still echoes on,
A call to arms for all womankind
To break free from societal bonds.
Her works, a beacon of hope and light,
Guiding us towards a brighter future,
A reminder that we too have the might
To make our voices heard, and be a culture.
Christine de Pisan, a pioneer,
Who paved the way for generations,
Her legacy, a legacy to cheer,
For all women to seek their aspirations.
She broke the mold and dared to be different,
A true inspiration for all, ever-present.
Her words, a legacy of power and strength,
A call to action for all, at any length.
For even though she lived in days of old,
Her message, still relevant, forever bold.
Let us honor her and keep her legacy alive,
For Christine de Pisan, truly did thrive.

# 22. Yuletide Descent: A Tragedy of U Bah from Bhoi

U Bah, from Bhoi, a man of impetuous and riotous mien,
Inclined to intemperate excess and remorse,
On one such Yuletide eve, he lurched forth from the tavern,
With but a single aim: a woman to bed.

In the streets of Shillong, his gait unsteady,
His inebriate mind fixated on base lust,
He encountered a female by the name of Ka Kong, with favors ready,
And without hesitation, with her did he entrust.

But as the nights progressed and he recurrently visited her,
His heart was ensnared in feelings for her,
Though she, with numerous men had been intimate before,
And to him, no affection did she proffer.

His family, aghast and disheartened, sought
To alter his mind, called for an organized prayer service with a priest
To pray for him to be away from sin,
But his passion was to no avail, they could not accept him.

As years gone by, he could not leave his family due to his attachment
to matrilineal society where he was the main Mama and had to take
care of his clan's legacy,
In solitude and whiskey, U Bah did reside,

His heart for her, a love unreturned, a final adieu.

And so, U Bah was left to dwell in solitude,
His love for Ka Kong, unrequited and true,
His heart forever bound by her allure,
And his passion, a fire that would not subdue.

For in the depths of his inebriate mind,
He could not shake the memory of her face,
The way she smiled, the way she laughed, entwined
With the longing of a love that could not replace.

But despite his family's disapproval and disdain,
He could not turn away from his own desire,
For in his heart, he knew that he would remain
Forever bound to her, a love set on fire.

U Bah lived his days in solitude,
His love for Ka Kong, forever unrequited, an interminable feud.

And as the years went by, his love for her
Did not diminish, but only grew more strong,
For in his heart, he knew that he would concur
Any obstacle, to make her his lifelong.

But alas, his love was not meant to be,
For Ka Kong, had moved on and found another,
Leaving U Bah, in despair to see
His love, unreturned, like a fallen lover.

But still, U Bah held on to his hope,
For the love that he had for her, was true,
And though she had moved on and let him go,
His love for her, would always renew.

U Bah's heart, it would not be denied,
For his love for Ka Kong, it burned bright,
And though his family and friends had sighed,
He knew that he would fight for her with might.

For in his heart, he knew that she was his,
His soulmate, his love, his guiding light,
And though she had moved on, and found another's kiss,
He knew that he would make her see the right.

And so, U Bah set out to win her heart,
With all the passion and intensity,
For in his mind, they were meant to be apart,
And he would do whatever it takes, to set her free.

But as fate would have it, his efforts were in vain,
For Ka Kong, had moved on, and never looked back again.

U Bah, did not let this defeat,
Bring him down, for he knew that he had tried,
And though his love for Ka Kong was incomplete,
He knew that he had to let go and move on, and decide.

So, he turned his focus to his family,
And the responsibilities that he held,
For as the main Mama, he had to be,
The one that his clan could rely on, and be compelled.

He took care of his family's legacy,
And worked hard to ensure their prosperity,
For even though his love was a mystery,
He knew that his duty was to his family, and not just his destiny.

Even as he dedicated himself,
To his family and their well-being,
His thoughts would often drift to Ka Kong, the delf
That he had once loved, and yearned for seeing.

But he knew that it was for the best,
To let go of his unrequited love,
For though his heart still ached with unrest,
He knew that it was time to look above.

And so, U Bah moved on with his life,
Though Ka Kong's memory still lingered on,
He knew that he had to let go of the strife
And focus on the things that truly mattered, and not just what was gone.

And as he looked back on his past,
He knew that he had made his peace at last.

# 23. The Elusive Quest: A Sonnet to the Omnipotent Creator

Omnipotent Creator, doth thou conceal
Thyself from mine eyes, which wide doth gaze
In fervent search for thee, my heart doth feel
A yearning deep, my mind doth seek thy ways

In this hour of need, I implore of thee
A sign of hope, a glimmer of thy grace
Forsake me not, O Lord, I beg of thee
Why art thou so elusive, hard to trace?

Though I confess, a sinner I have been
And not always lived a virtuous life
Yet in my heart, thy love doth reside within
And through thy teachings, I have sought to strive

But now, in this dire hour of despair
I am but a broken soul, in need of repair
My spirit doth ache, my heart doth rend
Why hast thou forsaken me, my closest friend?

Death doth beckon, an end to my pain
But in my heart, I know 'tis not thy will to sustain.

But what of the eternal laws of nature,
That govern the world with unchanging measure?
What of the mechanistic universe,
That spins on without mercy or pleasure?

In this grand scheme, we are but mere dust,
Subject to the laws that govern us,
And the Creator, if indeed there be one,
May not be the benevolent God we trust.

Perhaps it is our own will to power,
That drives us to seek solace and control,
And in the face of life's darkest hour,
It is our own strength that makes us whole.

For in the end, it is not fate or God,
But our own actions that shape our lives,
And in the face of death, we must applaud
Our own resilience and will to survive.

So let us not seek refuge in a deity,
But in ourselves, for therein lies true divinity.
Let us embrace our own mortality,
And find the strength to face life's adversity.

For in the end, it is not death that we fear,
But the thought of having lived a life without cheer.

And so, let us live our lives with purpose and intent,
Embracing the beauty and the pain that life brings,
For in the end, it is not the time we have spent,
But the memories we have created, that truly sing.

Let us not be slaves to fate or destiny,
But masters of our own path and destiny,
For in the end, it is not what is given to thee,
But what thou makes of it, that truly sets thee free.

Let us not seek refuge in illusions and myths,
But in the reality of our own existence,
For in the end, it is not the afterlife that we miss,
But the moments of our own lives, that hold true persistence.

So let us live our lives with passion and fire,
And embrace the beauty and pain, of life's mire.
For in the end, it is not the end that we desire,
But the memories of a life well-lived, that will never expire.

And let us not be swayed by the illusions of salvation,
Or the false promises of eternal life,
For in the end, our own actions and choices,
Are the only true means of ending strife.

Let us not be held captive by dogma and doctrine,
But let our own reason and understanding guide us,
For in the end, it is not faith that brings us redemption,
But our own actions and understanding, that truly enlighten us.

Let us not be afraid of death, or the unknown,
For in the end, it is not death that we should fear,
But the thought of having lived a life, alone,
And not having lived our lives, to the fullest, and with cheer.

So let us live our lives with purpose and meaning,
And embrace the beauty and pain, of life's fleeting being.
For in the end, it is not the end that we are seeking,
But the memories of a life well-lived, that will be our lasting being.

And let us not be held back by the constraints of tradition,
But let our own individuality and freedom reign,
For in the end, it is not the norms of society that bring us salvation,
But our own unique paths, and the choices we make, that sustain.

Let us not be blinded by the illusions of grandeur,
But let our own humility and wisdom guide us,
For in the end, it is not power and wealth that bring us honor,
But our own integrity and morality that truly sanctify us.

Let us not be afraid of change and uncertainty,
For in the end, it is not the known that we should fear,
But the thought of living a life without growth and diversity,
And not embracing the opportunities, that life holds dear.

So let us live our lives with courage and vigor,
And embrace the beauty and pain, of life's ever-changing figure.
For in the end, it is not the end that we seek,

But the journey of living a life, that is truly unique.

And let us not be held back by the shackles of conformity,
But let our own individuality and creativity flourish,
For in the end, it is not the standards of society that bring us harmony,
But our own unique perspectives and contributions, that nourish.

Let us not be swayed by the illusions of perfection,
But let our own imperfections and humanity guide us,
For in the end, it is not flawlessness that brings us connection,
But our own vulnerability and authenticity, that truly unite us.

Let us not be afraid of failure and vulnerability,
For in the end, it is not success that we should fear,
But the thought of living a life without risk and authenticity,
And not embracing the opportunities, that life holds dear.

So let us live our lives with authenticity and purpose,
And embrace the beauty and pain, of life's ever-changing discourse.
For in the end, it is not the end that we seek,
But the journey of living a life, that is truly unique.

# 24. Reminiscence of Imprisonment: A Sonnet

In carcerated chambers, where I spent my days,
I sought refuge in memories and ways
Of skies once brilliant and skies now gray,
And joys long lost in my familial glade.

But mostly, bitter memories consumed,
Each moment, as if they were part of me,
Since childhood days, when I was entombed
In feathers, and my soul began to see

The world's unfairness meted out to me,
And anger, when I realized my pain
Was not caused by my actions, nor by me,
But by external forces, I had no reign.

I sought to heal my wounds with love and care,
But infrequently, and found despair.
In search for normalcy and identity,
I felt a worthless incognito, free.

But then, I realized my soul was bound
In prison, of my own neural network found.
Where firing neurons led me to despair,
And powerlessness, I could not repair.

But then, one day, I crossed a bridge, where
Conscious met subconscious, light and air.
I found a cave, where wisdom was enshrined,
And monks had statues, from extremism mined.

A voice, like thunder, spoke, "I know why thou,
Art here, my son. What's past and what's ahead,
Is small, compared to what's within us now.
To be happy, forget how others led

You to pain, and focus on what you did
For others. The power lies within, my kid."
I unlocked the lock of inertia, and
Set myself free, through forgiveness grand.

Forgiveness, the key to unlock my mind,
A path to healing, that I had to find.
To let go of past hurts and move ahead,
And find true peace and happiness, instead.

And now, I see the world with different eyes,
No longer bound by memories and lies,
I live my life with purpose and with grace,
And find my joy in the human race.

For it's not in the past, nor in the future,
But in the present, where our souls mature.
And so, I'll take each step with care and pride,

And find my way, with my past in sight.

Though the sojourn may be arduous and long,
And the path fraught with tribulations,
I shall tread it with a steadfast heart and strong,
And in the end, find my tranquility and repose.

For in the ultimate analysis,
It is not the terminus that shapes our souls and nation,
But the journey that we undertake with diligence,
That forges us, and shapes our destinies, with elation.

For in the past, there were shadows and phantoms,
And in the future, there may be doubts and sorrows,
But in the present, there is strength and optimism,
And in the present, there is a panorama of opportunities to borrow.

For in the present, there is light and affection,
And in the present, there is guidance from the inner-self direction,
Thus, I shall take each step with care and pride,
And find my way, with my past in sight, and live my life, with all my might.

# 25. Ode to Sanguinity

In sacrosanct halls, where doctrine doth reign supreme,
Faith's virtue held in high esteem is derided,
For science deems it naught but an impediment vile,
A hindrance on the path to truth unbridled.

For facts and evidence, the savant
Examines with a frigid and calculating mind,
While faith, with its unshakable conviction,
In benightedness, prefers to stay confined.

But still, in both worlds, veracity is the goal sought,
In science, facts, in faith, the spirit's role,
Yet both in futility, for truth, a mirage fraught,
A will-o'-the-wisp, forever out of control.

For in the quest for knowledge and understanding,
We must recognize the limitations of our mind.

For science and faith, both have their own commanding,
And to choose one over the other is to be blind.

Thus, we must find equilibrium,
Between reason and faith, in our quest for truth,
For in this harmony, we shall find the equilibrium
And a path towards transcendence, our ultimate proof.

But still, the quest for truth is ever-elusive,
For facts and evidence are but one aspect of the whole,
Faith, with its unshakable conviction,
Provides a different lens, to see and to extol.

For truth, a multifaceted gem,
With many layers yet to be discovered,
And in this quest, we must not condemn,
But rather, let our minds be uncovered.

For in the end, both science and faith,
Are but tools, to aid us in our quest,
But it is the heart, that holds the key,
To understand and accept the rest.

For in this quest for truth, we must not be dogmatic,
But rather, open-minded and ever-inquisitive,
For in this, we shall find the pragmatic,
And the answers that we seek, will be revelative.

For truth is not a destination,
But rather, a journey, ever-evolving,
And in this, we must not be patient,
But rather, keep on moving.

For science and faith, both have their own merit,
And in this quest, we must not choose one over the other,
For they are but different paths, to the same spirit,

And in this harmony, we shall discover.

So let us not dismiss one for the other,
But rather, find balance, like a delicate feather.

For in the end, truth shall reveal itself,
And in this realization, we shall find our wealth.

# 26. Exasperation's Scourge: The Ineptitude Sonnet

Ineptitude, a scourge that oft doth bring
Misery and frustration, more than malice vile
For though malevolent intent may spring
From hearts of darkness, it can oft beguile

The mind, and be with reason reconciled
But those who lack the wit to comprehend
Are like a tempest, wild and undomesticated
Their simple minds, a constant demand

For effort, with no recompense in kind
Incentives such as wealth or carnal pleasure
Or accolades, to them are all blind
For they are vexatious beyond measure

Thus, in the realm of intellect and thought
Ineptitude is a more trying onslaught

For it is not malice that doth cause distress
But the lack of understanding and intelligence
And though it may be a trying test
We must strive to improve and make sense

Of the world around us and within

For it is through knowledge and understanding that we can truly
begin.

And in this quest for understanding and intellect,
We must not dismiss or look down upon
Those who may be deemed as intellectually inept
For they too have the potential to come along

For intelligence is not just about book smarts
But also about emotional and practical intelligence
And in this way, we can all make an impact
And strive for a better existence

So let us not be vexed by ineptitude
But rather, see it as an opportunity
To help others improve and to include
In the pursuit of knowledge and community

And as we strive for understanding and intellect,
We must not forget the importance of empathy
For it is through compassion and connection
That we can truly connect and be

Able to understand and relate
To those who may be deemed as intellectually inept
For in every person there is a innate
Potential for growth and to be adept

So let us not dismiss or look down upon

Those who may be deemed as intellectually inept
But rather, strive to help and include them in
The pursuit of knowledge and community

For in the end, it is not intelligence alone
But the willingness to learn, grow, and empathize that will bring us
home.

# 27. Reminiscence of Lost Youth

In contemplation of my youth departed,
Memories of days now past assail my mind
A melancholic pang within my heart is started
As I behold the young and all they find

In their juvenescence, a life of ease
That I in mine did not have the chance to know
Envy and jealousy within me seize
As I reflect on all that I did not know

I oft do ponder, had my youth been fair
Would I be a different person now?
A life of contentment and repose to share
Instead of emptiness that haunts me now

But alas, the past is immutable
And though it cannot be changed, I must be accountable
For my present and future, to strive
To help others find their way to thrive

Thus, I find solace in the betterment of others
As I come to terms with the memories of my youth, now passed and
covered.

And as I reflect upon my youth now gone
I must not dwell on what I did not have
For in the present, I have the chance to move on
And make the most of what I now have

For in every life, there are struggles and pain
But also, moments of joy and love
And it is through these that we gain
The strength to rise above

So let us not envy others their youth
For in the present, we all have the power
To create a life of meaning, and truth
In every single hour

For though the past cannot be changed
It is through the present that our future is arranged
Let us strive to make the most of now
And find contentment, peace, and a vow

To help others find their way to thrive
As we come to terms with the memories of our own youth, now passed
and bygone.

# 28. Triumph Through Perseverance: A Sonnet on Overcoming Adversity

Persevering through tribulation,
Encountering defeat, yet still moving on,
Engaging in strife, yet still evolving,
Undergoing metamorphosis, becoming strong.

For in the face of adversity, we grow
And through our struggles, we are truly tested
But those who push through, and do not let go,
Will find that victory is what they've invested.

For life is not a bed of roses, true,
But rather a path that requires much toil,
Yet those who persevere will see it through,
And find their strength and reach their goal's soil.

For in the face of tribulation,
We are not only tested, but also trained
For it is through our struggles, we find our own sensation
And in the end, our own potential is gained

And as we persevere through tribulation,
Let us not forget the importance of resilience

For it is through our ability to bounce back
That we truly transcend and become invincible

For in the face of adversity, we learn
To adapt and overcome, to find new ways
To not just survive, but to thrive and yearn
For growth and progress in all our days

And as we strive for victory and success,
Let us not forget the importance of compassion
For it is through empathy and kindness
That we truly make a difference and make a connection

So take the reins and fight, evolve, and strive
And in the end, triumph and fulfillment shall be thine.

# 29. The Onus of Benevolence: A Sonnet

In the progression towards our loftiest goals,
Assistance from another oft obtained,
But now, the onus lies upon our souls
To proffer aid to those who may be pained.

For as we ascend the stairway of renown,
We oft neglect the benefaction given,
But now, 'tis time to repay in like coin,
And offer aid to others, as in heaven.

For in this realm of travail, stress, and woe,
A benevolent act, a helping hand, bears weight,
It imbues the weary heart with hope and glow,
And lightens life's oppressive burdens freight.

For in the journey towards our aspirations,
We must not forget our obligations
To assist and empower others in their station
For in their success, our own true satisfaction.

So let us seize the reins and extend our hand in aid,
For in the act of giving, true success is made.

And as we strive to reach our pinnacle,

Let us not forget the importance of humility
For it is through the willingness to help others,
That we truly transcend and become fully

In the act of giving and proffering aid,
We not only assist others in their plight,
But also, we learn and grow, and evade
The dangers of becoming self-absorbed and spite.

For true success is not only measured in fame,
But also in the impact we make on others
And it is through the act of giving and being humane
That we can truly call ourselves successful brothers

So let us strive for our loftiest goals
But also, let us proffer aid to those who may be pained and in woes.

And as we proffer aid to those in need,
Let us not forget the importance of respect
For every individual is unique indeed,
And their struggles and journey are to be kept

In mind as we offer our assistance
For in giving aid, we must not impose
Our own ideals, but rather provide a balance
And empower them to find their own path and chose

For true success is not only measured in fame,
But also in the impact we make on others

And it is through understanding and empathy, our aim
That we can truly assist and empower others

So let us strive for our loftiest goals
But also, let us proffer aid to those who may be pained and in woes,
with respect and understanding as our roles.

# 30. Botanical Fortitude: The Jeanne Baret Sonnet

In circumspection of laws, Baret set sail
With naturalist Commerson by her side
To Bougainville, a distant, verdant isle
Their journey fraught with perils, deep and wide

Disguised as man, "Jean" Baret traveled far
With botany dreams in her heart's desire
But fate would soon reveal her secret star
And thrust her into a tempestuous fire

Upon the island, she led with great skill
Collecting plants of rare and wondrous kind
But tragedy struck and her heart did fill
With grief and sorrow, of a love unblinded

Though her journey was fraught with woe and pain
Her legacy lives on, in botany's gain.

Though Baret's name was lost to history
Her pioneering work, a botanical mystery
Her discoveries, a treasure trove of flora
Her legacy, a testament to her honor

For she braved the seas and overcame the odds

To bring forth knowledge, to the world of botanists' gods
Her name, forever etched in the annals of science
A trailblazer, a true botanical alliance

In the remote isle of Bougainville, she found
Species of plants, rare and profound
Her work, a cornerstone for future generations
Her legacy, an inspiration for botanical explorations

So let us remember Jeanne Baret, a true botanical heroine
Whose legacy lives on, in the world of botanical flora.

Though her journey was beset with adversity
Her spirit and determination, never falter
Her botanical discoveries, of great rarity
A testament to her knowledge, and her valor

For Baret, the sea was her ultimate stage
Where her passion for botany, she could engage
Through the treacherous storms and the rough seas
She persevered, with a heart full of botanical breeze

For Baret, the island of Bougainville was her destiny
Where she could uncover the secrets of botanical history
Her legacy, a treasure trove of botanical diversity
A true inspiration to all, in botanical curiosity

So let us raise our glasses, to the memory of Jeanne Baret
A true botanical pioneer, who shall never be forgotten.

# 31. Realms Unveiled: A Sonnet on Proprietorship and Autonomy

Upon assuming proprietorship o'er one's fate
And abstaining from vocalization of plight,
Ascend to the heights of autonomy,
And discover portals hitherto unknown.

With fortitude and steadfast determination,
Embark upon the path to self-sovereignty,
Braving the trials that beset the nation,
And vanquishing the obstacles with dignity.

For true autonomy is not granted,
But earned through trials and tribulations,
And those who undertake the journey, enchanted,
Shall find the doors of opportunity waiting.

No longer bound by fate or circumstance,
But master of one's destiny, it's true,
To seize the opportunities that chance
And open up a world of possibility anew.

So seize the reins of fate with steadfast hand,
And navigate the seas of life with grace and command,

Forge a path of self-determination,
And ascend to the pinnacle of self-realization.

With unwavering resolve and steadfast will,
Embrace the journey of self-discovery,
And transcend the shackles of fate and thrill,
Of charting a course to true autonomy.

For in the pursuit of self-governance,
We unlock the secrets of our own existence,
And gain the power to shape our own chance,
With the freedom to make our own persistence.

So let us not be swayed by external force,
But let us be the masters of our own fate,
And in the face of life's tumultuous course,
Let us rise above and dominate.

For in the end, true autonomy,
Is the key to living life authentically,
And in this quest for self-sovereignty,
We shall find true fulfillment and tranquility.

# 32. Eminence Through Effort: A Sonnet on the Process of Attainment

Attainment of preeminence is not a task to be undertaken lightly,
For it necessitates arduous labor and exertion,
And the acquisition and practical application of knowledge, which can prove uneasy,
To successfully navigate the tempestuous vicissitudes of life.

Elevation to a position of dominance is not for the indolent intellect,
But rather for those who actively seek, endeavor, and educate themselves,
Through every encounter and circumstance, both favorable and adverse,
In order to continually advance and improve.

For success is not a terminus, but rather a perpetual journey,
Requiring incessant cultivation and expansion of one's capabilities,
And through each step and every educational experience,
The full extent of one's potential is revealed.

Thus, seize the reins of your own development,
And steadfastly pursue knowledge, and the fruition of your aspirations shall be yours to reap.

But do not mistake the attainment of eminence
As the ultimate goal of life's journey,
For true fulfillment lies not in fame or wealth,
But in the cultivation of one's inner harmony.

The pursuit of knowledge and self-improvement,
Should be driven not by external validation,
But by a desire for personal enlightenment,
And the betterment of one's fellow human nation.

For true success is not a destination,
But a journey of self-discovery and growth,
A path that leads to inner liberation,
And the attainment of a harmonious whole.

So let not the pursuit of eminence consume,
But rather, use it as a means towards wisdom and inner bloom.

And remember that the road to eminence,
Is not without its share of obstacles and strife,
But with perseverance, determination,
And the guidance of a moral compass in life,

One can overcome any hindrance,
And reach the summit of one's aspirations,
And in the process, gain a sense of transcendence,
And find true meaning in one's vocation.

For eminence is not an end in itself,

But a means to a greater purpose,
A tool to be used for the betterment of oneself,
And the betterment of all in the world's surface.

So strive for eminence with a noble heart,
And use it to bring about a better start.

# 33. The Proclivities of Prosperity: A Sonnet of Habits and Success

The habits that thou dost cultivate,

Shall shape the course of thy success,

For they can accelerate or abate,

The path to greatness, with finesse.


The choices made each day, are not apart,

But integral to thy grand design,

For habits, be they virtuous or tart,

Shall shape the future, in a line.


The journey to glory may be fraught,

But with habits virtuous, it shall be smooth,

And in the end, the fruits of labor, nought,

But a testament to wisdom, truth.


So let the habits be chosen with care,

And let them shape the future, with a flare,

For in the cultivation of habits fair,

Lies the key to success, beyond compare.


And in the face of adversity,

Let not the spirit falter or be bent,

For in the cultivation of stoic tenacity,
Lies the path to victory, unspent.

So let the habits be chosen with resolve,
And let them guide the way, with steadfast will,
For in the cultivation of self-control,
Lies the path to greatness, and the thrill.

And let not the burden of habit weigh,
Upon the mind, or cause despondency,
For though the path may be long and strait,
The rewards of perseverance shall be.

In the face of challenge and strife,
Let not the spirit falter or decay,
For in the struggles of this mortal life,
Lies the path to ultimate victory.

Let the habits be met with fortitude,
And the obstacles with determination,
For in the pursuit of one's own latitude,
Lies the path to true self-realization.

And let not the mind be swayed by ease,
For true success comes not without toil,
But through the cultivation of discipline and perseverance,
Shall the path to glory, be made fertile.

And in the end, when the journey is done,

When the struggles have all been fought,
The rewards, shall be bountiful and won,
For the habits, were steadfast and taught.

So let the habits be chosen with care,
And let them guide the way, with prudence,
For in the cultivation of habits fair,
Lies the key to success, with abundance.

And let not the future be feared,
For with habits virtuous and stoic resolve,
The path to glory, shall be cleared,
And the future, shall be yours to evolve.

So let the habits be steadfast and true,
For in them lies the key to all that's due,
The cultivation of habits, shall renew,
The path to success, and the future, anew.

# 34. Purposeful Progression: A Sonnet on the Fear of Death

'The ineluctable approach of mortality,

Should not engender in the mind, a sense of anxiety,

But rather, the neglect to realize

The ultimate goal of our transient existence.


For death, the ultimate outcome of our being,

Is but a termination of our earthly tenure,

However, an existence of significance and meaning,

Is what we should all strive to ensure.


Therefore, let not death be the focus of your dread,

But rather, an existence devoid of contemplation and purpose,

For time is ephemeral, and opportunities fleeting,

Easily missed if one's attention is not directed.


Thus, embrace the present, and make the most,

For in the final analysis, that is what truly matters and will boast.


And let not the transience of life's duration,

Cause you to neglect the quest for self-improvement and cultivation,

For in the pursuit of knowledge and self-discovery,

Lies the path to true fulfillment and serenity.


Let not the fear of death obscure your vision,

But rather, use it as a catalyst for decision,
To live a life of virtue, integrity, and purpose,
And leave behind a legacy of honor and worth.

For in the grand scheme of things, our time is but a fleeting instant,
A mere blip in the vast expanse of existence,
But in that brief moment, we have the power to create,
A legacy of significance that will forever resonate.

So, fear not death, but fear living without purpose,
And strive to make the most of every single surface.

And let not the brevity of life's sojourn,
Cause you to neglect the pursuit of truth and learning,
For in the quest for wisdom and understanding,
Lies the path to true enlightenment and transcendence.

Let not the shadow of death, obscure your sight,
But rather, use it as a reminder to do what's right,
To live a life of compassion, kindness, and grace,
And leave behind a legacy of love, that will endure in every place.

For in the end, it is not the length of our days,
But the depth and breadth of our impact in ways,
That will determine the worth of our existence,
And secure our place in the annals of posterity.

So, fear not death, but fear living without love,
And strive to make the most of every moment above.

# 35. Examining the Grandiloquence of Wagner's Opus: A Philosophical Perspective on the Human Condition

In Tolstoy's russian lexicon, one may peruse
The name of Wagner, a composer of great renown,
But his opus, a mere palliative to diffuse
The agony and lamentation of the world all around.

His compositions, grandiose and sweeping, possess
Potent force, yet with motifs of jingoism and loathing,
His heritage, a mirror of humanity's most sordid excess,
And a reminder of our innate state of depravity, and woeing.

His art may be grandiloquent, yet the cost
Of disregarding the harm his ideologies engender,
Is one that shall forever be forever lost,
When pondering his legacy, we ought to remember.

For all aesthetic and art is but a delusory mirage,
A transient refuge from the incessant enigma,
A mere diversion from the eternal anguish,
That is our existence, forever in vain.

But still, we seek solace in the beauty of art,
For in the chaos of life, it is a beacon of heart.

It may not solve the enigma of our existence,
But it gives us a moment of transcendence.

Yet, in the end, art can only provide a temporary respite,
A fleeting refuge from the mundanity of life,
A mere illusion to distract from the plight,
Of the eternal enigma, that is our strife.

For though Wagner's compositions may be grandiose,
They are but a mere palliative to the human condition,
A fleeting distraction from the eternal woes,
And the existential questions of our disposition.

But still, we seek refuge in the beauty of art,
For in the chaos of life, it is a beacon of hope,
A moment of transcendence, where we can depart,
From the mundanity of life, and learn to cope.

For art, though it may not provide the answers,
It gives us the courage, to face the enigma that is existence.

Thus, we must not dismiss Wagner's opus,
As mere palliative, to the human plight,
For in his compositions, we may find a focus,
A way to confront, the eternal night.

For though his ideologies may be flawed,
His art remains a testament to the human spirit,
A reminder that in the darkest hour, we can applaud,
The resilience, that lies within it.

But still, we must not forget, the cost,
Of disregarding the harm, his ideologies engender,
For in the end, it is what shall forever be lost,
When pondering his legacy, we must remember.

For art, though it may not provide the answers,
It gives us the courage, to face the enigma that is existence,
And in this quest, we must not lose sight,
Of the moral compass, that guides our persistence.

For art, though it may not provide the answers,
It gives us the courage, to face the enigma that is existence,
And in this quest, we must not lose sight,
Of the moral compass, that guides our persistence.

Thus, we must examine Wagner's legacy,
With a critical eye, and a discerning mind,
To separate the beauty from the malignancy,
And discern, what is of worth, to humankind.

For though his compositions may be grandiose,
They are not a panacea for the human plight,
But rather a reflection of our complexity and woes,

And a reminder of the eternal night.

So let us not dismiss Wagner's opus,
But rather, let us learn from it, and gain insight.

And in this examination, we shall come to see,
The complexities of humanity, and our destiny.

# 36. Genuine Greatness: A Sonnet on the Elusiveness of Authenticity

Authenticity, a virtue of elusive nature,
An ideal oft-ignored and overlooked,
In the quest for conformity, we forsake
And lose ourselves in the quagmire of imitation.

But to emulate another, is to betray one's essence,
For true distinction and eminence reside in our idiosyncratic form,
Embrace your peculiarities, gifts, and assets,
And in the realization of one's individuality, flourish.

For veracity is the foundation of true greatness,
And authenticity is the key to liberation,
No longer constrained by societal conventions,
But to live truly, authentically, and with exuberance.

Therefore, seize control of your own identity,
And be true to yourself, for in genuineness, brilliance will flourish and
flourish.

And as you journey on the path of authenticity,
Remember that it is not a destination,
But a continuous process of self-discovery,

And the continuous cultivation of self-integration.

For authenticity is not about pleasing others,
But about being true to oneself,
It's about embracing one's own unique colors,
And not being afraid to stand out and be oneself.

It's about the courage to be different,
And to be true to one's own values and beliefs,
It's about the willingness to take risks,
And to live life on one's own terms, with no griefs.

Authenticity is not easy, but it is worth the pursuit,
For in being true to oneself, one finds true contentment and fruition.

And as you strive to live authentically,
Do not forget to extend compassion and empathy,
To others who also seek to live true to themselves,
For in our shared humanity, lies true unity.

Authenticity is not a solitary pursuit,
But a collective journey towards self-discovery,
It is about respecting and honoring diversity,
And embracing the unique qualities of each and every.

For in embracing the authenticity of others,
We also embrace our own, and in doing so,
We create a world where everyone can be true to themselves,
And live a life that is truly fulfilling and whole.

So let us strive for authenticity with compassion and empathy,
And in doing so, we shall bring about a brighter reality.

# 37. Dhanushkodi : A Sonnet

In southernmost India, where land and sea
Conjoin in a desolate, ghostly town,
A place where no man doth remain, but be
Left with ruins, tattered and brown.

The confluence of the calm, blue Indian Ocean
And the green, choppy Bay of Bengal, doth make
A sight both beautiful and in motion,
But the abandoned town doth nothing but ache.

For all that once was, is now lost and gone,
A reminder of man's ephemeral fate,
The ruins, a symbol of what we have done,
A testament to our innate hate.

This ghost town, Dhanushkodi, is a place
For those seeking solitude, a silent space.

# 38. Nostalgia for the Lost Self: A Sonnet of Self-Reflection

Of all the souls that cause my heart to ache,
And all the losses that I've had to bear,
None holds such weight as the one I forsake,
Myself, my being, my true self so fair.

For in the past, a different human being I knew,
With aspirations, ideals, and all that life can give,
But now that self is lost, and I pursue,
A shadow of the man that I once lived.

And though I strive to find myself again,
In memories, in dreams, in hopes and fears,
My former self remains just out of range,
A ghost, a recollection, a disappearing tear.

And so, of all that I've lost, I miss,
Myself the most, in this, my heart doth bliss.

For in the quest for self-discovery,
Let not the mind be swayed by illusions,
For true understanding and mastery,
Lies beyond the realm of mental confusion.

So let the mind be stilled and at ease,
And let the self be observed with equanimity,
For in the understanding of the self, true peace will be found,
And true self-realization, will be attained with serenity.

And let not the mind be burdened by regrets,
For in the release of the self, true liberation will set,
And the path to self-realization, will be met,
In the cultivation of self-awareness, forever to last.

So let go of the past and embrace the self,
And find true peace and self-realization, in the self.

And let not the mind be clouded by doubts,
For in the understanding of the self, true wisdom will sprout,
And the path to self-discovery, will be found,
In the cultivation of self-awareness, without a doubt.

And in the face of adversity,
Let not the spirit falter or be bent,
For in the cultivation of self-acceptance,
Lies the path to self-realization, unspent.

So let the mind be open and free,
And let the self be observed with detachment,
For in the understanding of the self, true peace will be seen,
And true self realization, will be attained with detachment.

And let not the mind be consumed by fears,
For they are but shadows, without substance,
But the true self, is the one that appears,
In the stillness of the mind, it takes wing.

So let the mind be open and free,
And let the self be observed with detachment,
For in the understanding of the self, true peace will be seen,
And true self-realization, will be attained with detachment.

# 39. The Ambition's Paradox: A Sonnet of Grandiose Aspirations

Thou shouldst set thine sights on goals so great,

That thou doth not know how thou shalt achieve,

But trust in thine own strength, and fate,

And know that thou shalt find a way to weave.


A path to reach the dreams thou doth desire,

Through trials, doubts and fears that may assail,

For only then, thou shalt truly aspire,

To reach the heights, where true glory doth unveil.


Thy ambition, should be grand and bold,

So terrifying and yet exciting too,

For in the quest, lies tales yet untold,

And greatness that in thine future, doth grew.


So let thy heart be filled with fear and hope,

And chase the dreams that make thy heart elope.

# 40. The Conundrum of Ethanol's Quantitude: A Sonnet of Salubrity

I doth not know the names of those who should,
This wisdom hear, and take it to their heart,
But this I know, that health oft doth require,
A abstinence from ethanol depart.

The optimal amount for well-being's sake,
Is none, a number most detrimental,
For those who seek to healthful lives awake,
This truth should be most evidential.

But still, I know not who doth need to hear,
This message, sent to guide and to inform,
But if perchance it doth fall on an ear,
That needs the guidance, let it not be scorned.

For health is wealth, and none should it forsake,
And ethanol in naught doth health partake.

And in the quest for self-preservation,
Let not the mind be swayed by temptation,
For true understanding and preservation,
Lies in the abstinence from fermentation.

So let the mind be guided by reason,
And let the self be controlled with discipline,
For in the forsaking of ethanol, true health will be gained,
And true self-preservation, will be attained with diligence.

And let not the mind be burdened by regret,
For in the abstinence from ethanol, true liberation will be set,
And the path to self-preservation, will be met,
In the cultivation of sobriety, forever to last.

So let go of the ethanol and embrace health,
And find true self-preservation, in sobriety and wealth.

And let not the mind be clouded by doubts,
For in the forsaking of ethanol, true wisdom will sprout,
And the path to self-preservation, will be found,
In the cultivation of sobriety, without a doubt.

And in the face of adversity,
Let not the spirit falter or be bent,
For in the cultivation of self-discipline,
Lies the path to self-preservation, unspent.

So let the mind be guided by principles,
And let the self be controlled with restraint,
For in the forsaking of ethanol, true health will be regained,
And true self-preservation, will be attained with restraint.

And let not the mind be consumed by fears,

For the temptation of ethanol is but a fleeting thing,

But true self-preservation, is the one that appears,

In the cultivation of sobriety, it takes wing.


So let the mind be guided by reason,

And let the self be controlled with discipline,

For in the forsaking of ethanol, true health will be regained,

And true self-preservation, will be attained with diligence.

# 41. The Paradox of the Mind: A Sonnet of Self-Realization

The thoughts that flit through thy mind, dear one,
Are not the essence of thy being, true,
For thou art but the observer, not the sum,
Of the thoughts that shape thy world anew.

The more one comprehends this truth profound,
The easier it is to disengage,
From thoughts that bind and cause such heart-wound,
And free thyself from each oppressive cage.

For thoughts, though constant, oft-times are not true,
And hold no weight in the realm of existence,
To know this truth, is to see thoughts anew,
And free thyself from their oppressive persistence.

So let the thoughts go, and be who thou art,
Embrace thy true self, free from mental art,
For in the release of thoughts, doth start,
The journey towards true peace of heart.

And in the face of adversity,
Let not the mind be swayed by thoughts unkind,
For in the cultivation of stoic tranquility,
Lies the path to self-discovery, unblinded.

So let the thoughts go, and be who thou art,
And find true peace, in thyself, deep in heart.

And let not the mind be enslaved by thoughts,
For they are but fleeting and ephemeral,
But the true self, is the one that's sought,
And lies beyond the realm of thought.

And in the quest for self-discovery,
Let not the mind be swayed by illusions,
For true understanding and mastery,
Lies beyond the realm of mental confusions.

So let the mind be stilled and at ease,
And let the thoughts drift away like leaves,
For in the release of the mind, the true self will be freed,
And true peace, shall be found within the heart, with ease.

And let not the mind be burdened by doubt,
For in the release of thoughts, true wisdom will sprout,
And the path to self-realization, will be found,
In the cultivation of mindfulness, without a doubt.

So let the thoughts go, and be who thou art,
And find true peace, in thyself, deep in heart.

And let not the mind be consumed by fears,
For they are but shadows, without substance,

But the true self, is the one that appears,
In the stillness of the mind, with a sense of reverence.

And in the quest for self-mastery,
Let not the mind be swayed by distractions,
For true understanding and clarity,
Lies beyond the realm of worldly actions.

So let the mind be focused and clear,
And let the thoughts be observed with equanimity,
For in the control of the mind, the true self will appear,
And true peace, shall be found within the heart, with serenity.

And let not the mind be burdened by regrets,
For in the release of thoughts, true freedom will be set,
And the path to self-realization, will be met,
In the cultivation of mindfulness, with no regrets.

So let the thoughts go, and be who thou art,
And find true peace, in thyself, deep in heart.

And let not the mind be ruled by desire,
For it is but a fleeting thing,
But the true self, is the one that's higher,
In the stillness of the mind, it takes wing.

And in the quest for self-enlightenment,
Let not the mind be swayed by illusions,
For true understanding and transcendence,

Lies beyond the realm of mental conclusions.

So let the mind be open and free,
And let the thoughts be observed with detachment,
For in the release of the mind, true self will be seen,
And true peace, shall be found within the heart, with detachment.

And let not the mind be burdened by the past,
For in the release of thoughts, true liberation will last,
And the path to self-realization, will be cast,
In the cultivation of mindfulness, forever to last.

So let the thoughts go, and be who thou art,
And find true peace, in thyself, deep in heart.

# 42. The Time-bound Harvest: A Sonnet of Effort and Reward

In the laborious exertions of this moment,
Lies the promise of a bountiful return,
For in the toils of now, power is impotent,
But soon the compounding wheel shall churn.

Two years hence, when the labors have been wrought,
A pivotal moment shall be at hand,
Opportunities then, shall be besought,
Without cause for lament or reprimand.

For in the work that is undertaken,
Lies the seed of a bountiful future yield,
And as time passes, effort not forsaken,
Shall bring growth, both bountiful and real.

Let the efforts be steadfast and true,
For in them lies the key to all that's due,
For the labor of the present, is the rue,
Of a bountiful future, yet to accrue.

Thus let the toils of now, be not in vain,
For they hold the power to break the chain.

And let not the burden of effort weigh,
Upon the mind, or cause despondency,
For though the path may be long and strait,
The rewards of perseverance shall be.

In the face of adversity and strife,
Let not the spirit falter or decay,
For in the struggles of this mortal life,
Lies the path to ultimate victory.

Let the endeavors be met with fortitude,
And the obstacles with determination,
For in the pursuit of one's own latitude,
Lies the path to true self-realization.

So let the efforts be steadfast and true,
For in them lies the key to all that's due,
The labor of the present, shall renew,
The bountiful future, that's yet to accrue.

And in the face of uncertainty,
Let not the mind be clouded with fear,
For the future, though unknown, holds many a possibility,
And with efforts, it can be made clear.

So let the journey be embarked upon,
With a spirit of perseverance and will,
For in the efforts of the present, a new dawn,

Shall break forth, and the future fulfill.

And in the end, when the labors are done,
When the struggles have all been fought,
The rewards, shall be bountiful and won,
For the efforts, were steadfast and taught.

So let the efforts be steadfast and true,
For in them lies the key to all that's due,
With labor and perseverance, a new view,
Shall be gained, and the future, renewed.

# 43. Passion's Reticence: A Sonnet on the Importance of Prudent Speech in Times of Ire

Behold the virtue of circumspection
Amidst the tempest of ire's eruption,
For in thy passion, reason may depart,
And lead to utterances, that thou shalt regret,
When thou hast regained thy composure,
And cleared thy troubled heart.

In moments of intense anger, thy emotions
May cloud thy judgment and lead to mistakes,
And actions thou shalt later come to rue,
For words spoken in haste, are oft deceits.

Embrace the stillness of equanimity,
Ere thou dost engage in discourse or make decisions,
For in a state of calm, thy mind shall see,
And thou shalt avoid future revisions.

Therefore, let thy words be measured and discreet,
And thou shalt not be ensnared by error's heat.

So let not the fervor of thy ire
Consume thy reason and thy will,
For in its grip, thou mayst set fire
To bridges, that thou later shalt feel ill.

Thus, practice restraint, and hold thy tongue
When passions rise, and tempers flare,
For in a state of calm, thou art strong,
And wisdom's voice, thou shalt hear.

In discourse, let thy words be chosen,
With care and thought, and not in haste,
For in a state of calm, thou art frozen,
And errors, thou shalt not taste.

So let thy heart be still, and serene,
And in thy words, let wisdom be seen.

# 44. The Vigilant's Discretion: A Sonnet on the Preservation of Friendships

Vigilant discretion should be employed,
If e'er your words may cause a friendship's fall,
For friendships are a treasure to be enjoyed,
And should be held in high esteem by all.

But recklessness or impetuosity,
Can cause irreparable damage to a tie,
Thus, circumspection must be exercised,
To keep the bond from being sundered nigh.

Let prudence be the guide by which we speak,
And circumspection govern all our words,
For language, wielded thoughtlessly, can wreak
Havoc upon the heart and leave deep girds.

Thus, let our tongues be tempered by the mind,
And weigh each utterance with care and grace,
For words, once spoken, cannot be confined
And may inflict upon the heart a wound that trace.

But if we guard our words with circumspection,
And speak with prudence and discretion,

Our friendships shall remain in perfect reflection
And flourish in a state of sweet fruition.

So let us not be rash in what we say,
But measure each word, and choose them well, each day.

And let us not forget the power of words,
To shape our thoughts and shape the world around,
With every phrase and every sentence heard,
We shape the narrative that we have found.

Thus, let our words be chosen with great care,
For they have the power to both harm and heal,
To build or to destroy, to show we are aware,
Or to reveal our ignorance and zeal.

For in the end, our words will be our legacy,
A reflection of the wisdom we have gained,
And how we choose to use them, will be key,
In shaping the world and the lives we've sustained.

So let us speak with purpose, and with thought,
And leave behind a legacy that will not be bought.

And let us not forget the power of silence,
In which the truest wisdom often lies,
For in the stillness, we can gain compliance
With the inner voice that guides us to the skies.

Words are not always necessary,
Sometimes, it's better to let them be,
For silence can be a form of dignity,
And in its stillness, we can truly see.

So let us use our words with great intent,
And when the time is right, let us refrain,
For in the balance, true enlightenment
Will be found, and wisdom will remain.

Thus, let our words be measured, well-conceived,
And let our silence speak louder than our words, achieved.

And let us not forget the power of words,
In the written form, they have the power to last,
Through the ages, they can be heard,
And their meaning, forever will be cast.

In literature, poetry and prose,
Words can paint a picture, tell a tale,
And leave an impact that forever glows,
In the minds of those who read and prevail.

So let us take care with what we write,
For our words will be remembered long,
And in the pages of history, the light
Of our message will continue to belong.

Thus, let our words be measured, well-conceived,

In both speech and writing, let them be perceived.

And let us not forget the power of words,
In the realm of politics, they can sway,
The masses and create a new world,
Or lead to chaos and decay.

Words have the power to unite or divide,
They can create a nation or destroy,
It is crucial that they are used with pride,
And with a sense of purpose, not a toy.

Thus, let our words be measured, well-conceived,
In the arena of politics, let them be clear,
And let our intentions be well-perceived,
For the future of the nation is at stake, my dear.

So let us use our words with great care,
For they have the power to shape the world we share.

And let us not forget the power of words,
In the realm of art, they can inspire,
Elevate the soul, and give it wings,
And set the imagination on fire.

Words, when blended with melody and rhyme,
Can create a symphony of sound,
And transport us to a different time,
And leave us spellbound.

Thus, let our words be measured, well-conceived,
In the realm of art, let them be true,
And let them flow with a rhythm and a beat,
And let them speak to me and you.

So let us use our words with great skill,
For they have the power to create beauty still.

As we continue to use our words,
Let us remember the impact they can have,
On ourselves and those around us,
For they are a powerful tool to grab.

In every situation, great or small,
Let us choose our words with care and thought,
For they can build or they can fall,
And their effects can be long sought.

Let us strive to speak with kindness,
And let our words be a reflection of our hearts,
For when we speak with positivity,
We can play our part in making a better start.

So let us use our words with intention,
And let them be a force for good, in every dimension.

# 45. Verbose Discretion: A Sonnet on the Importance of Prudent Speech

Abstain from garrulity, if thou dost lack

The full account, for in thy hasty speech,

Misconceptions may be born, and errors stack,

And thou shalt be the cause of much besmirch.


Verbalizing ere the whole tale is told,

Is like to bring about much confusion,

And lead to judgments, that are rash and bold,

And cause much harm, with no just resolution.


Therefore, let thy tongue be still and mute,

Till thou hast heard the tale in its entirety,

And then and only then, shall thou dispute,

And form conclusions with sobriety.


So let thy words be measured, and discreet,

And thou shalt not be caught in error's heat.

# 46. The Reticent's Caution: A Sonnet on the Power of Words

Observe reticence if thy words may transpire
To cause offense or hurt to another's soul,
Be cognizant of the impact they'll acquire,
And weigh them well, ere they leave thy lips whole.

Be mindful of the repercussions they'll bring,
And how they'll shape the thoughts of those around,
For words are powerful, and can cause a sting,
And leave deep wounds, that may never be unbound.

If thou art uncertain if thy words may be,
Misinterpreted, causing harm or pain,
It is advisable to maintain thy glee,
And keep thy tongue, from uttering them in vain.

So let thy words be measured, and discreet,
And thou shalt not be caught in error's heat.

# 47. Eloquent Reticence: A Sonnet on the Importance of Temperate Speech

In moments of discourse, when passions rise
And tempers flare, it's easy to lose sight
Of rational thought and civilize
And let our tongues engage in verbal fight.

In such moments, let us not be swayed
By impulses that lead to altercation
But instead, let us seek a calmness, a shade
And let our words be spoken with moderation.

For in the heat of argument, we see
Only the flaws in our opponent's stance,
But in the silence, we gain clarity,
And find new ways to enhance our discourse.

Thus, when discourse turns tempestuous,
Let us abstain from vocalization,
And seek a state of mind auspicious,
Where speech is clear and calm, not quick to lash out in frustration.

And when serenity and calm we find,
We can return to discourse, peace of mind,

And with clear thoughts and open mind,
We can find solutions, and be serene and kind.

For in discourse, true wisdom lies,
And through peaceful discussion, we can grow,
And gain new perspectives, new ties,
And learn from those with whom we disagree, and know.

But in order to gain this wisdom,
We must first learn to control our tongues,
And speak with reason and freedom,
And not let emotions get the better of us, among.

For it is only through civil discourse
That we can truly understand
And reach a common ground, of course,
And find solutions that benefit all, and expand.

So let us strive for calm and clear expression,
And engage in discourse with discretion,
And find in each conversation, a new lesson,
And reach a state of understanding, with no division.

# 48. The Pecuniary Privation: A Lesson in Lucidity and Mindfulness

In the crucible of pecuniary privation,
I discovered that my cogitations,
Were overly preoccupied with the vexation
Of financial stress, a fruitless fixation.

With the realization came a newfound lucidity
That my emotional energy was squandered,
In a fruitless endeavor, a futility,
Leaving me with a sense of being impounded.

I realized that I was expending
Inordinate amounts of psychical energy,
On a matter of little import, a misapprehending
Of the true nature of my adversity.

Amidst the scorching flames of penurious plight,
My self-conceit was purged and brought to heel,
For in the crucible of fiscal distress,
Arrogance, a hindrance, had to be quelled.

Through humility's embrace, I was schooled,
And learned to seek the counsel of my peers,

For in the tempest of economic woes,
Collaboration, the key to allaying fears.


Thus, I relinquished the stronghold of my pride,
And discovered in humility, true resilience,
For only through relinquishing command,
Could I attain true growth and abundance with imminence.


With sagacity and perspicacity,
I gleaned the import of fortitude and tenacity,
In the midst of pecuniary adversity,
It is facile to relinquish, to forgo fortitude.


But I apprehended that genuine felicity,
Is not quantified by material accretion,
But by the aptitude to surmount adversity,
And to persevere through tribulations, to persist.


Hence, I cultivated perseverance,
And to persist in my endeavors,
For in the face of financial severity,
Perseverance is the key to progress.


For in the ultimate analysis, true opulence,
Is not solely about pecuniary means,
But about the richness of existence, and the journey.

# 49. Champions of Obscurity: A Sonnet of Gratitude and Remembrance

Commemorate not the individuals who bore witness to thy presence,
During the juncture in which thou were obscured by others' eyes,
For they were steadfast in their belief, and did not waver,
Even when thou were invisible, they did not desert or vacillate.

Their unwavering support, a testament to their fortitude,
Was a beacon of hope amidst the darkness, and a guiding light,
Their steadfastness, in the face of thy obscurity,
Was a shining example of loyalty and friendship, truly bright.

These individuals, though oft-overlooked, deserve our gratitude,
For they were there, in thy hour of need, and did not flinch,
Their unwavering support, a source of strength and fortitude,
Deserves to be remembered, in each and every inch.

So let us not forget, these champions of our past,
Whose support, in our darkest hour, did truly last.

# 50. The Sonnet of Penurious Peril

The penurious circumstance, a state
Of pecuniary destitution dire,
Wherein one's finances are abate
And financial means are but a mire.

The privation of the means to acquire
The necessities of life, doth bring
A sense of inadequacy, a fire
Of insecurities, a gnawing sting.

The indigence of coin doth oft engender
A feeling of inferiority,
A sense of being a pauper, a lender
Of shame and worthlessness, a malady.

But in this state of fiscal privation,
We learn the value of resourceful adaptation.

And though we may feel the weight of poverty
Bearing down upon us with its force,
We must not let it defeat our dignity
And rob us of our strength and resource.

For in the depths of penury's despair

Lies the seed of determination,
A spark of hope that can repair
The wounds of destitution's erosion.

With frugality and ingenuity,
We can transcend the limitations
Of our monetary scarcity
And find success in our aspirations.

So let us not despair in our penury,
For it is through adversity that we find our true worth and quality.

For in the face of pecuniary plight,
We must not lose sight of our own might.
For though we may be poor in wealth,
We are rich in spirit and in health.

We must not let our finances define us,
For we are much more than our bank accounts.
We are the sum of our experiences,
And our worth cannot be measured in amounts.

So let us rise above our penurious state,
And strive for greatness in all we do.
For though we may be poor in finances,
We are rich in the currency of perseverance and virtue.

In the end, it is not wealth that defines us,
But the way we face and overcome our struggles and difficulties

# 51. Tenacity Triumphant: A Sonnet of Resolve and Persistence

Triumph shall be mine, though not with fleetness, yet with inevitability
With persistence and fortitude, I'll vanquish all adversity
My resolve, unyielding as adamant, shall see me through
For I am imbued with a tenacity, that nought can subdue

Perseverance, my stalwart ally, shall guide me on my quest
Through tempests fierce, and mountains steep, to ultimate success
For though the path may be beset with obstacles, I'll not falter
With constancy, my goal I'll reach, and victory will be my alter

Nay, I'll not be swayed by doubt, nor cowed by failure's sting
For I am blessed with a spirit, that's unbounded and unbroken
And though the journey be long, and the road arduous
Triumph shall be mine, in the end, and glory shall be my reward, thus.

# 52. Epistolary Ode to Valor and Amour

Thine embodiment doth tell thy sole behest,
Begin thou to scribe thine opening stanza forthwith,
Endow thine epic with deeds of valor and love,
And fill it with felicity, ere it ends.

Let each verse be a testament to thy quest,
A chronicle of thine heroic deeds,
A tale of amorous adventures at their best,
A saga of thy life, and all it proceeds.

Let every rhyme sing of thy courage and might,
Of passions that burn with a fierce intensity,
Of joys that make life a beautiful delight,
And sorrows that make it a bitter enmity.

So let thy existence be thy grand discourse,
A masterpiece of literature, without remorse.

# 53. The Amorous Fervor: A Sonnet of Passion and Tranquility

When first I beheld thy visage, my love, so fair,
My heart was ensnared by its beauty rare,
A passion deep and true, beyond compare,
Filled me with fervor, an amorous flare.

With trembling hands and nervousness profound,
I acted like a billy goat, so bold,
In hopes to make my feelings truly found,
And win thy love with aroma, so bold.

But in the face of my trepidation,
I sought refuge in my chambers still,
To calm my nerves and find salvation,
And attain a state of tranquil will.

But now, my love, I see thee once again,
And all my fears and doubts are put to end.
For in thy eyes, I see my future bright,
And know that you are the one I'll hold tight.

For in thy presence, I am truly alive,
And my heart sings with joy and energy.

For you are the one that makes me thrive,
And fills my life with love and harmony.

And so, my love, I vow to always be,
A faithful and devoted lover to thee.

For in thy love, I find my true identity,
And my purpose in life is made clear to me.
And so, my love, I'll hold on tight,
And cherish you forever, day and night.

And though the future may be filled with uncertainty,
I know that with you by my side, we'll find serenity.

For in thy love, I find my true self,
A reflection of my deepest desires,
And in thy embrace, I find my wealth,
That quenches the thirst of my soul's fires.

And though the journey may be long and rough,
I'll walk it hand in hand with you,
For in thy love, I find enough
To face any challenge that comes through.

For in thy love, I find my ultimate truth,
A connection that transcends all youth.
It's an inexplicable sensation,
A profound and eternal revelation.

With thee, my love, I find my sanctuary,
A safe haven from the world's malignancy,
With thee, my love, I find my destiny,
A purpose that enlivens my vitality.

# 54. The Symphony of Resilience: A Sonnet of Lamentation and Perseverance

Lamentation doth befall all lives, a plight,
A vexation that doth cause the heart to ache,
Yet in this misery, a beacon bright,
Doth shine, a way to heart's wounds to undertake.

The sole method of perseverance doth lie
In capering to one's symphony of buoyancy,
A dance with rhythm that doth make us fly,
And lift us from our lamentation's malignancy.

For in this symphony of positivity,
We find the strength to face each day anew,
And in the dance, a sense of true humility,
Away from vexation and towards virtue.

So let us dance, and find within the beat,
Perseverance, and a life complete.

# 55. Euphoric Adoration: A Sonnet of Eternal Love

With every gaze, my heart doth leap,
As I behold thy visage so sublime,
A love so unsullied, so complete,
A treasure that shall forever gleam.

When first we met, my nerves were aghast,
But in thy presence, I found my repose,
A love that shall forever last,
To cherish, honor and never oppose.

With every caress, my soul doth ignite,
A flame that burns with ardent light,
A love that shall forever unite,
And guide us through the murkiest night.

Thus let us waltz beneath the firmament,
And murmur endearments in each other's ear,
For in this love, we have found,
The most invaluable boon life doth bear.

This love, a thing of beauty rare,
A bond that time and distance cannot sever,
A symphony of passion, a love affair,
A treasure that we shall cherish forever.

With every breath, my heart doth sing,
As I bask in thy love's radiance,
A love that is a perfect wing,
To soar above life's turbulence.

With every step, my soul doth soar,
As we journey through life's winding path,
A love that is forevermore,
A guiding light, a beacon of hope and faith.

So let us dance to love's sweet tune,
And bask in its eternal light,
For in this love, we shall find our boon,
And bask in its eternal delight.

This love, a thing of sublime art,
A masterpiece, a work of beauty and grace,
A bond that nothing can tear apart,
A treasure that shall forever endure and embrace.

With every heartbeat, my soul doth swell,
As I bask in thy love's glorious shine,
A love that is a tale to tell,
A story of love, passion, and divine.

With every step, my spirit doth rise,
As we journey through life's winding way,
A love that is a paradise,

A haven, a refuge, a shelter for us to stay.

So let us dance to love's sweet melody,
And bask in its eternal warmth,
For in this love, we shall find our destiny,
And bask in its eternal charm.

# 56. Empyreal Triumph: A Sonnet of Inner Demons and Love's Healing Power

In the labyrinthine corridors of the psyche,

We wage a war against the demons of the past,

To find within the heart a solace that's unique,

And heal the wounds that once did make us aghast.


But in this battle for the soul's deliverance,

We find that fortitude and tenacity prevail,

For though the path may be both dark and dreary,

With love as guide, our efforts will not be frail.


For love, the noblest virtue, doth imbue

Guidance and light in our journey to transcend,

And in its effulgence, our fears subdue,

And all our scars, both physical and mental mend.


And as we face the demons of the mind,

With love as armor, we shall be divinely inclined.


And in this quest for inner redemption,

We must trust in the power of love's persuasion,

For it is the key to unlock our salvation,

And find the strength to win this eternal fight.

And though the demons of the mind may try,
Love will guide us to victory and the light.

For love is the ultimate elixir,
That gives us strength to transcend and to conquer,
And in its embrace, we find deliverance,
From the demons that once did us encumber.

So let us trust in love and its might,
And find the strength to win this endless fight.

For love is the ultimate transcendence,
A state of being that elevates the soul,
It's the key to unlock the gates of existence,
And find the meaning that makes us whole.

It is the force that drives us to evolve,
To rise above our fears and our despair,
To find the courage to seek and resolve,
To find the will to heal and to repair.

It is the light that shines in the darkness,
Guiding us through the trials of life,
It's the beacon that guides us to the starkness,
And shows us the path that leads to the light.

It's the ultimate philosophy,
That teaches us to live with humility and empathy.

And in this battle for the soul's redemption,
We must trust in love's power and intention,
For it's the key to unlock our liberation,
And find the strength to win this endless fight.

So let us trust in love and its might,
And find the strength to win this endless fight.

# 57. The Luminous Horizon of Hope

Wrapped in a veil of serenity,
Alone in the home, with all for solace,
But a voice on the phone, to bring harmony,
As clouds part in a bright and auspicious brace.

The skies brighten to a radiant, azure hue,
As lightning strikes, illuminating the day,
The earth beneath quivering, as if to renew,
As winds whisper and sing in a peaceful sway.

Though nature's tempest may rage with fury,
And bring destruction to all in its path,
We must not forget the beauty and wonder,
That surrounds us, in the aftermath.

For in the chaos and turmoil, we find,
A chance to rebuild, to grow, and to refine.

And as the rain begins to pour in a deluge grand,
On screens, the news shows images of hope,
Cyclonic storms bring new life to the land,
In spinning paths of rejuvenation they cope.

But we must not despair, for in the end,

The sun will rise, and hope will never end.

For in the darkness of the tempestuous night,
Lies the seed of a new and brighter light.

And though the present may be filled with pain,
The future holds the promise of gain.
And so, we must remain optimistic,
For in the end, that is truly authentic.

For in the face of adversity,
We discover the true strength of our resilience.
And through our struggles, we may find solace,
In the realization of our own perseverance.

So let us trust in the power of hope and love,
And find the strength to rise above.

For in the face of nature's tempestuous might,
We must remember the beauty of its light.
For though the storm may bring destruction and pain,
It also brings new life, growth, and rejuvenation.

And so, we must embrace the change,
And find the courage to rebuild and to renew.
For in the aftermath of the tempest,
Lies the opportunity for growth and breakthrough.

And as we face the challenges of life,

We must remember that hope will always survive.
For in the darkest of moments,
There is always a glimmer of light that will revive.

And so, we must embrace the power of optimism,
And find the strength to rise above the chaos and adversity.
For in the end, it is our attitude,
That determines our ultimate destiny.

So let us trust in the power of hope and love,
And find the strength to rise above,
And in the end, we shall find peace,
In the tranquility of the soul's repose.

# 58. The Enchained Heart's Lament

Though I with utmost diligence do strive,
To cast off bitter chains that bind my soul,
My life, with all its sorrows, doth survive,
And I in fetters, like a prisoner, roll.

For what protracted term must I endure,
Without the freedom to my heart's desire,
And smile, a thing that seems forever pure,
But now, alas, forever out of mire.

Existence proves too formidable a foe,
To be subdued by mortal's puny might,
And so I'm trapped in bitter misery's woe,
With no escape from this perpetual plight.

But still I hope, that one day I'll be free,
And all my sorrows, vanished, I shall see.

# 59. The Amorous Lunacy: A Sonnet of Salvation and Poesy

When Cupid's dart transfixes thy breast,
And thou art caught within the web of love,
Thou mayst discover thyself at behest
Of madness, driven by the gods above.

But fret not, for there is a remedy
For thy disturbed psyche, oh my dear;
The quest for poesy, the artistry
Of adoration and aesthetic cheer.

It shall be thy salvation, thy release
From Cupid's grasp, and elevate thee high
To the esteemed rank of poet laureate,
A title earned through verse and eloquence.

So let thy pen be guided by the muse
And find solace in the beauty of verse.

# 60. The Enigma of Self: A Ponderous Musing

My cerebrum oft doth with ponderous musings teem,
As I ponder upon my very essence.
Who am I? Why am I in this world supreme?
These queries I reiterate with persistence.

My raison d'etre, I do oft seek to discern,
And ruminate upon this mortal plight.
My identity, a conundrum unconfirmed,
A quandary that I endeavor to enlight.

This quotidian quest doth exact a toll,
But still I seek the answers I crave.
Though oft my thoughts are muddled, and not whole,
I'll not relinquish, until my soul is saved.

So let me ponder, let me seek and yearn,
Until my questions find a final turn.

# 61. The Fervent Attraction: A Sonnet of Amorous Passion and Tranquility

When first I espied thy countenance fair,
Upon thy entry to the hall of youth,
My heart was seized with passion rare,
And filled with fervor of amorous truth.

I trembled with a nervousness profound,
Acting in madness, like a billy goat,
In hopes of making my affections found,
By exuding an aroma to promote.

But in the face of my trepidation,
I sought refuge in my chambers still,
To calm my nerves and find salvation,
And attain a state of tranquil will.

But now, my love, I see thee once again,
And all my fears and doubts are put to end.

Thou art the light that guides me through the dark,
The beating heart within my chest that sings.
With every step I take, my love for thee doth hark,
A symphony of passion, joy, and wings.

Thy beauty, like a rose in full bloom,
Enchants my senses and my soul doth stir,
With every glance, my love for thee doth consume,
A fire that burns with passion, fierce and pure.

Thy touch, like a gentle summer breeze,
Brings calm to my tumultuous soul,
With every kiss, my love for thee increases,
And makes my heart complete and whole.

My love, thou art the one I've been searching for,
My heart is yours forever, now and evermore.

# 62. The Beguiled Heart: A Sonnet on Love's Disappointment

In endeavors all, there's naught that doth compare
To love, in terms of hopes that are invested.
With grandiose expectations, we ensnare
Our hearts, yet oft our love is uninvested.

Forsooth, in all the undertakings, nay
None doth so oft in failure termination.
As love, which doth with such high hopes begin,
Yet ends in disappointment and lamentation.

Thus doth the heart, with eager hopes beguiled,
Find disappointment, as love's dreams are thwarted,
And all the while, the soul is left beguiled
By love's illusions, which so oft are thwarted.

But though love oft doth end in disappointment,
Yet still the heart doth in its hope's anointment.

# 63. The Enigmatic Harmony: A Sonnet of Nongriat's Bifurcated Root Bridge

Bridgeways woven from arboreal roots profound,

Exemplify the Khasi's bond with earth,

The descent to Nongriat's bridge astound,

Commencing at the peak of valley's girth.

With every step, a natural splendor found,

A panorama of beauty and worth,

The root bridges of Meghalaya's ground,

An enigma, part of ancient Khasi mirth.

Navigating rivers wild and woods so dense,

Was routine in days of yore long past,

Nongriat's bridge unique, a grand defense,

Against the rushing waters, built to last.

Rock-encircled pools for rest and repose,

And food to nourish, after arduous woes.

# 64. Umbrella of Strength: A Sonnet on Facing Fears and Insecurities

Existence, a maleficent dreamscape wrought,
Where trepidations and apprehensions dwell,
Incessantly plagued by fear and loathing fraught,
Akin to one who brandishes an umbrella well.
Due to a phobia of the deluge of my being,
I oft am ignorant of the precise object of my dread,
But still, I live my life in constant fleeing,
From all the things that keep me trapped in bed.

But still, I hope for a brighter morrow,
Where fears and insecurities will flee,
And I'll find peace, without any sorrow,
And live my life, with all my heart and glee.

So let me take this umbrella in my hand,
And face the rain, with all my strength and stand.

# 65. Smit's Splendor: A Sonnet on the Intertwining of Nature and Culture

Amidst the verdant countryside of Smit,
A place of botanical wealth and grandeur,
Where culture and tradition interknit,
And the 'iing-sad' holds royal grandeur.

The Nongkrem Dance, a yearly affair,
Is held in the halls of traditional kings,
Where dancers sway with grace and flair,
Their movements, like the flutter of wings.

But Smit is not just culture and tradition,
It's also home to a natural wonder,
The grandiose chasm, Laitlum, with its fusion
Of grassy plateaus, and a deep asunder.

Trek down to the valley settlements below,
Or stand on the edge, and watch the water flow,
And let the natural beauty of Smit,
Envelop your senses, and leave you in wit.

# 66. The Posthumous Altruism Sonnet: "A Gift to Nature's Cycle"

When fate doth visit with its fateful scourge,
And death's remorseless hand doth me assail,
Let not my mortal form be interred,
But rather, let my vital organs serve
As instruments of life's perpetuation,
That another may partake of nature's boon.
Leave my remains to repose in sylvan dell,
To be by fauna and the flora consumed,
Thus fulfilling the eternal cycle,
And in death, a new existence resumed.

Let not my passing be in vain, but rather,
Let my demise yield a beneficent end,
For in the ultimate analysis,
It is not wealth nor fame that truly matter,
But the lives we've touched and the love we've shared.

So when I go, let this be my final plea,
Donate my organs, that another may live and be.

Let my physical demise be the catalyst,
For a new beginning, a new lease on life,

For someone in dire need of vital organs,
My death a boon, an act of sacrifice.

Let this be my legacy, my final quest,
To give the gift of life, to be at rest.

Let not my death be in vain, but rather,
A means to an end, a noble endeavor,
For in the grand scheme of things,
It is not our wealth, nor fame that truly matters,
But the impact we make, the love we share,
So let my death be a catalyst,
For another's life, for that I shall be grateful.

And let my passing be a reminder,
Of the fragility of life and our mortality,
And the importance of organ donation,
For it is a selfless act of humanity.

Let my death be a call to action,
For others to consider organ donation,
For in giving the gift of life,
We can transcend our own mortality.

And in this way, my legacy shall live on,
Through the lives of those who receive my organs,
And my death shall not be in vain,
But rather, a continuation of life's cycles.

Let my passing be a contemplative thought,
For us to ponder on the meaning of life and death,
For in the end, it is not the length of our days,
But the impact we make that truly matters.

So when fate doth visit with its fateful scourge,
And death's remorseless hand doth me assail,
Let my passing be a celebration of life,
And a reminder of the beauty of selflessness.

And let my death be a reminder too,
Of the interconnectedness of all things,
For in giving the gift of life to another,
We are a part of the eternal cycle of being.

Let my passing be a reminder,
Of the importance of empathy and compassion,
For in understanding the plight of others,
We can truly make a difference in this world.

Let my death be a call to action,
For us to strive for a better world,
Where all have equal access to life-saving resources,
And where organ donation is the norm.

Let my passing be a reminder,
Of the power of love and selflessness,
For in giving of ourselves,
We can truly make a positive impact on the world.

So when fate doth visit with its fateful scourge,
And death's remorseless hand doth me assail,
Let my passing be a tribute to life,
And a call to action for a better world.

# 67. Assertive Authenticity: A Sonnet of Self-Discovery

I bid adieu to pleading for my essence fair,
For confrontation is my second skin,
And candor, my tongue doth oft declare,
Though curt it may, it speaks of truth within.

If thou doth seek to tarnish my good name,
I shall with impudence, yet courteous, reply,
For I am tired of playing this game,
Of molding self to please the passerby.

I'll be myself, unbridled and unbound,
And let my true self freely be expressed,
For why should I in meekness be renowned,
When all I seek is to be truly blessed.

I'll stand for self and for my rights I'll fight,
For in myself, my true worth takes flight.

# 68. The Epiphany of Lentils: A Sonnet of Sovereignty

In ancient realms of kings and queens,
Where power was the paramount means,
The people lived in servitude and fear,
Bowing to their rulers, year by year.

But in this land, there lived a valiant few,
Who dared to dream of something more, something new;
They knew that true strength lay not in gold or throne,
But in the epiphany of simple things unknown.

And so, with due diligence and propriety,
They learned the art of lentil-ingestion, and set free
Their minds and souls from shackles of subservience,
Ascending to a state of true self-reliance.

For in the act of partaking thus,
They showed their strength, their will, their very soul;
A symbol of their courage, honor, and trust,
A sign that they were whole.

And thus, with lentils in hand, they stood tall,
Defying kings and rulers, one and all;
For in this simple act, true strength resides,
And with it, the power to claim their rightful prize.

So let us all partake in lentils with pride,
For in this simple act, true strength resides,
And with it, the power to rise and strive,
To be free, and to claim our rightful lives.

# 69. The Paradox of Insanity: A Sonnet of Sovereignty

Without a tinge of irrationality,
One's audacity shall be wanting,
For to sever the shackles of conformity,
One must dare to take a leap of faith.

In the confines of rationality and sanity,
We are but vassals to societal conventions,
But with a semblance of madness, we can perceive
The true path to autonomy and transformation.

For to liberate ourselves from the bonds that confine,
We must embrace the unknown and the unpredictable,
And with a intrepid heart and a receptive mind,
We can break free from our self-imposed penury.

Thus, let us not dread the madness within,
For it is the key to true sovereignty.

# 70. Trials Triumphant: A Sonnet of Fortitude and Resolution

With fortitude and steadfast resolution,
Embrace the trials that life doth present;
For in the toil and tribulation,
Lies the key to sweet success' ascent.

Let difficulty be thy lever,
To lift thee up and lead thee to the stars;
For in the face of life's endeavor,
Lies the path to victory's bright bars.

So soar ahead, with courage in thy heart,
And in the struggles of this mortal sphere,
Find solace and a path that doth impart
The means to vanquish all thy doubts and fear.

For in the end, 'tis not the easy way
That leads to glory's bright and shining day.

# 71. Elysian Wanderings: A Sonnet to the Sylvan Glades

Oh, lead me to the sylvan glades profound,

Where gentle hand in mine is firmly clasped,

And we shall stray among the trees renowned,

Whose ethereal presence doth outlast


The fleeting years, and all the winds that blow.

Escort me to the heart of wildwood prime,

Where soothing melody doth overflow,

From babbling brook, cascading through the time


Of tranquil peace, and gentle rustling breeze

That whispers through the branches overhead.

Take me to solitude where mind at ease

Can find repose, as droplets on a leaf that's shed


From heavens above. A realm where man holds nought

But nature reigns supreme and all is brought

To harmony, where soul is truly caught.

# 72. The Beauty of Mohini

Mohini, fair celestial being of pulchritude and allure,
Renowned for her beguiling and alluring countenance,
The personification of beguilement, her arm
Can lead the hearts of mankind in any circumstance.

Personification of enticement, she
The mistress of passion, her every gesture
Awe-inspiring, captivating, untamed and free
She leads the hearts of mankind to their rapture

With every glance and every step she takes,
She leaves a trail of broken hearts in her wake
Her beauty is a weapon, her love a serpentine
That coils around and hearts, it doth make hearts ache

But still we worship at her feet, in awe
Of Mohini, goddess of unbridled amour.

# 73. Logotherapy : A Sonnet

In logotherapy's potency doth lie
The means to bestow upon the troubled mind
A sense of purpose, and the fortitude to ply
Life's tempestuous and trying paths confined.

For those who, in despondency, had sought
Escape in death, it grants a newfound drive
To strive, to endure, to surmount and outwrought
The trials that life's exigencies contrive.

For logotherapy does not impart
A transient hope, but rather imbues
The inner self with steadfastness of heart
To vanquish life's adversities and rues.

Thus, to the troubled, logotherapy
Affords a chance for life's continuance, and victory.

# 74. Lunaris Fortitudo

Amidst my idiosyncrasy, not unlike the lunar force
Whose strength doth ebb and flow the ocean's tide
But on its surface, naught of weight it can enforce
Not even the astronaut who doth abide

I am capable of lifting others high
And giving aid to those who need it most
But when it comes to bettering myself, I sigh
For in that task, my power is a ghost

Thus, like the moon, my strength is not complete
It waxes and wanes in its own paradox
For while I am able to lift others' feet
My own I cannot lift from this abyss

But still, I strive to better and improve
For in that quest, my strength shall truly groove.

# 75. Cognitive Fortitude

The world is fraught with trials and tribulations,
A field of battle where each must take their stance.
But let us not in the face of such vexations
Yield to defeat, but learn to adapt and enhance.

Let us improvise, and exert our cerebral might,
To surmount each obstacle that doth impede.
For with each challenge overcome comes insight,
And fortitude to face the next with greater speed.

For life is not a game of fate, but art,
Where those who master strategies and ploys
Will rise above the fray and claim their part,
And seize their opportunity to employ.

So let us not in the face of challenges cower,
But rise and conquer them in every hour.

# 76. Perdurable mettle

Though tempests rage and gloom surrounds,
And fate doth seem to deal a blow,
I'll not succumb to fear profound,
For in my breast, a strength doth grow.

Through trials fierce, I'll onward press,
With head held high and heart of steel,
For I am master of my fate,
And captain of my soul to wield.

Though winds may howl, and waves may dash,
I'll not be swayed by fate's wild tide,
For I am more than flesh and bone,
With spirit strong and will unbridled.

So let the world unleash its might,
I'll stand unfaltering in the fight.

# 77. Kudle beach : A Sonnet

Nestled near Gokarna's picturesque town,
A sanctuary for those who seek repose,
The pristine and spectacular Kudle beach,
Is idyllic, a place where one can compose

The mind and flee the cacophony of life,
And find serenity in nature's bower,
The long-shore, of golden sands, doth provide
An idyllic setting in each tranquil hour.

The sunset viewed from this strand, is grand,
Nothing short of spectacular to behold,
The relative lack of crowds, doth enhance the land,
Making the experience manifold.

So if you seek a tranquil, peaceful retreat,
Where nature's beauty is yours to meet,
Kudle beach is the perfect place, discreet.

# 78. Pondicherry : A Sonnet

During my youthful days, I had the chance
To reside in a land replete with charm,
Known for its amiable, languorous trance,
And French colonial architecture, grand.

Pondicherry, a place that's much sought after,
A popular attraction, it doth prevail,
Despite its fame, it's still a place of laughter,
Where one can find tranquility, exhale.

With picturesque townships, such as Auroville
And majestic beaches, like Promenade,
It's the perfect place for those who will
Escape the chaos, and find peace, to evade.

With amiable weather and serene ambiance
It's an ideal destination for those in a trance.

# 79. Tosh : A Sonnet

Tosh, a village of aesthetic grace,
Enshrined in the verdant Parvati dale,
Renowned for panoramic vistas that trace
The serene ambiance that doth prevail.

This idyllic hamlet, lush and verdant,
Enveloped by the cascade's misty veil,
And graced by peaks that snow-capped preen,
Is the perfect haven for those who assail

The frenetic pace of modernity
With the desire to immerse in nature's bower,
A leisurely stroll doth serve as a key
That invigorates and keeps one from dower.

But for a truly transcendent experience,
One should seek out lodging with a view immense,
And spend their time in meditative trance,
Basking in beauty's sublimity, intense.

# 80. Hampi : A Sonnet

Hampi, a land of ancient ruins, doth take
One back to a time of grandeur and pride,
Where rubies and diamonds once did grace
The streets, and gold and silver were currency, a tide.

But such grandeur is but a fleeting thing,
A mere shadow of what once was great,
For in the end, all that remains is the fling
Of man's ambition, a bitter fate.

The peace and simplicity it offers,
Is but an illusion, a fleeting dream,
For in the end, all that truly suffers
Is man, lost in his own self-esteem.

Hampi's ruins, a reminder of our fate,
A testament to the human state.

# Just For You

We thank you, dear reader, yes you,

For taking the time to read this book through,

A masterpiece of words, a journey true

Of understanding humanity, it's what we do.

We hope you've gained something, a newfound view

Of life, of love, and all that is so new.

For completed reading this book, we're so glad,

That you've joined us on this journey, so mad

About life, love, and all that we've had,

A chance to explore the depths, to be glad

To be a part of this journey, so glad,

To understand the heart of humanity, a part so sad.

Do read other books from the Homo Sapiens series,

A journey of words, a path to find the truth,

To understand what makes us human, so true

Our hearts intertwined, a love so pure and bright,

A thirst for knowledge, a quest for what is right,

A journey of reflection, a search for the light.

And other books by the same author too,

A journey of words, a path of discovery,

The secrets of life, the wonders of the world,

A journey to understand, a quest for truth,

The author's voice, a guide to our journey,

A journey to enlightenment, a path to our destiny.

We thank you, dear reader, yes you,

For reading this book, for making it through,

A masterpiece of words, a journey of truth,

We hope you've gained something, a newfound view,

Of life, of love, and all that is so new,

Do read other books from the Homo Sapiens series, a journey true.

Warm regards,

A - Team

P.C : Clarissa Candace Giri

Meet Mawphniang, a man of many parts,
A lawyer, entrepreneur, and more,
With boundless curiosity, and open heart,
And a passion for life, that he will explore.
With talent, drive, and a thirst for success,
He has achieved much, in the professional sphere,
But it is in writing, where he finds the best,
And where his true passion, shines so clear.
With boundless curiosity and verve,
He embraces new ideas, with an open mind,
And ventures boldly, into unknown lands,
With fearlessness, that is truly one of a kind.
From Syadheh Village, in Ri Bhoi District,
He hails, a soul ever-striving, never at rest.
And as he writes his story, with fearlessness,
He makes the most of every moment, ever-unfurled.
And though his journey, may take many roads,
Each step, a step toward self-discovery,
With every word, he shares his soul's abode,
And invites us all, to join in, and be.
For Mawphniang, life is a precious gift,
To be cherished, and explored, with all one's might,
And as he writes, he lifts, our spirits, and uplifts,
With tales of wonder, and delight.
So let us follow, this soul ever-striving,
And be inspired, by his boundless energy,
For Mawphniang, is a man truly thriving,
In a world, that he makes, all the more lovely.

And as we read, his words, so full of life,

We too, shall be, forever, changed by his strife.

And though his journey, may be filled with strife,

He never loses sight, of what is true,

For he knows, that in the end, it is life,

That gives us meaning, and a purpose too.

And so, he writes, with a heart full of love,

And a mind, that is always seeking more,

For he knows, that in the depths, of the dove,

Lies the answers, to life's great riddle, and score.

And as we read, his words, so full of grace,

We too, shall be, forever, touched by his pen,

For Mawphniang, is a man, with a gentle face,

And a heart, that is always, filled with love again.

So let us cherish, this soul ever-striving,

And be inspired, by his boundless energy.

Warm regards,

A - Team

# Note

*As I, a breviloquent raptor, wield A lever, with naught else to my design, I generate tones for the aural field In this prosaic orb we call mankind. My actions, though, are but a small part Of forces far beyond my control, For nature holds the key to each chart And sets the laws that govern the whole. But still, I am compelled to explore The workings of this vast machinery, To seek the truth that lies at core And find the answers to humanity. Though some may call it quest I'll seek the truth, with no time to rest.*

*Author*